Praise

Framing Success

"Leslie McIntyre-Tavella's story is as incredibly inspirational as it is instructive. This book is a powerful business-building blueprint, teaching us all how to do well by doing good."

—**ALEX GOLDFAYN,** *Wall Street Journal* bestselling author of *5-Minute Selling*

"This candid, practical, personal book captures the essence of the entrepreneurial life and how business leaders can thrive in a fast-changing world. Every aspiring and experienced entrepreneur can benefit from McIntyre-Tavella's hard-won wisdom."

—**MARK C. PERNA,** speaker, CEO, and award-winning author of the bestseller *Answering Why: Unleashing Passion, Purpose, and Performance in Younger Generations*

"*Framing Success* provides a powerful blueprint with inspiring examples, practical tools, and tested techniques for renovating your business. It will help you transform your business into one that reflects professionalism, character, and achievement. This is a perfect gift for the new business owner; a great refresher for a seasoned one."

—**CHIP R. BELL,** author of *Inside Your Customer's Imagination*

Framing Success

20

Essential Lessons for

Achieving Entrepreneurial

Greatness from a

Self-Made Multimillionaire

LESLIE McINTYRE-TAVELLA

AN INC.
ORIGINAL

An Inc. Original
New York, New York
www.anincoriginal.com

This work is being published under the *An Inc. Original* imprint by an exclusive arrangement with *Inc. Magazine*. *Inc. Magazine* and the *Inc.* logo are registered trademarks of Mansueto Ventures, LLC. The *An Inc. Original* logo is a wholly owned trademark of Mansueto Ventures, LLC.

Distributed by River Grove Books

Design and composition by Greenleaf Book Group
Cover design by Greenleaf Book Group

Publisher's Cataloging-in-Publication data is available.

Paperback ISBN: 978-1-7360283-4-6

Hardcover ISBN: 978-1-63909-000-6

eBook ISBN: 978-1-7360283-5-3

First Edition

To my husband,
who followed my every
whim and filled every jar,
and to my darling daughter,
the cherry on top of it all.

Contents

Acknowledgments

Our "small but mighty" family consists of my devoted husband, Ralph, "the glitter" of our family, and our daughter, McKenzie. Without their support, compassion, insistence, and humor, this book might not have come to fruition. McKenzie, you bring me my greatest sense of accomplishment and joy. Knowing that we raised a compassionate, kind, independent, strong-willed, pragmatic woman who will continue my mission of guiding others to become the best they can be fills me up every day. You are truly my legacy, my greatest achievement, and a constant source of joy.

To my husband, Ralph: my loving, kind, loyal, and trusted partner of thirty-two-plus years who tolerates my every whim, listens to every idea, fills every jar, and has run toe to toe with me for three decades, it wouldn't have been nearly as special without you by my side. I truly picked a "winner" when I chose you. And me, well, I've been told that I am the "glue" always holding things together, completing our "small but mighty" family unit.

To my partner Tom, thank you immensely for filling in all of my gaps, for your fortitude and unwavering belief in our company, your encouragement, patience, and abundance of love and kindness. You will always and forever be my one and only work partner.

To my dearest friends, Todd, Lisa, Jennifer, Joann, Mark, Prisco, and Gina, and my dearest Diana, who has been with me through most of my life journey—I thank you for your love, sharing your families with ours, your humor, your knowledge, and everything that each of you has taught me. Each of your successes, failures, views, and values has added to our families and made us who we are today.

To my Renaissance Executive Forum family, I thank you for your tough love, honest feedback, brilliant insights, support, and kindnesses. Each of you are entrepreneurial heroes getting up every morning to fight another day, to sustain and grow your businesses to be the very best that you can be. I am eternally grateful for your friendship, love, and boundless support.

To my mentors: Marian and Phil McIntyre; Michael Mulcahy, past president of Trans-Lux Corporation; and Robert Pfann, each of whom inspired and encouraged me to be better by sharing their lessons in life and business. And finally, to Art Papas, who over dinner one night asked me about my story and told me it was worth sharing. *You* have been inspirational and a role model, showing me how to be an incredible leader and treating me as though I was always your most important customer!

And to Al Trebing, my counsel and dear friend of twenty-five-plus years: You have been my guiding light, always available for me day and night, propping me up when I needed support, pushing me when I needed encouragement, and guiding me when I became lost and couldn't quite find my way. Without your guidance, patience, knowledge, and mentorship, this journey might not have ended as it has. Thank you for sometimes knowing me better than I know myself.

And finally, to my birth family and siblings: It was no easy journey, but the "glimpse" of a better life was available to me because of it. I am deeply grateful for the tough lessons afforded me when I was young so that I developed the grit, fortitude, and determination to choose a different and much better life for myself.

Special appreciation and gratitude to Anaka Mastrianni for being invaluable with her ideas, wit, and youth beyond years. You are truly an amazing young woman who came to me at a time when I needed you most!

Preface

Running a small business for thirty-plus years afforded me a lot of learned lessons. Business starts and ends with the customer—acknowledging, honoring, appreciating, and pleasing the customer—in every single interaction. I've spent a lot of time speaking to customers about their experiences and what they truly want in a business partner. In business today, being good is merely the entry fee. In order for your business to continue and thrive, you must be consistently exceptional. Everyone talks the same talk—but few walk the walk! Managers and C-level executives are busier than ever these days, being bombarded by meetings and chats, emails, text messages, social media, and so on. It is the duty of leaders to help them cut through the clutter and noise and deliver a superior experience and product repeatedly and consistently.

When I was twenty-two years old, I started my own business when all odds were stacked against me. You see, I did not finish high school or attend college. I have an eleventh-grade education. I had a very unsettled home life and was eager to start out on my own, knowing I could only depend on one person—me.

At a young age, I had the unique opportunity to get a "glimpse"—that is, a glimpse of two lifestyles I could choose for myself. I lived in two extremely different household environments for many years, which allowed me to clearly see the long-term consequences of both. Bouncing back and forth between an abusive, unpredictable, and addiction-filled home and a loving, nurturing, and supportive one gave me a very clear illustration of what kind of life I could have when I set foot on my own path.

My mother returned to work three days after I was born, which placed me securely in the hands of my godmother, Marian McIntyre, and into a home filled with wonderful smells and nurturing, kind people. Aunt Marian was a person who would eagerly sit on the floor and play *Candy Land* for hours at a time, happily neglecting most of her household chores or other impending tasks.

But at home, my siblings and I witnessed some very ugly behavior and many dark events, things that children shouldn't have to see or survive. My sister, who died a few years ago from alcoholism and other self-inflicted complications, was forever haunted by our childhood. My brother, who is still alive today, probably endured even more than I did, and perhaps the worst of us all; ultimately, he was the one who always tried to protect my mother from the fallout my father brought home every night.

By the grace of God, I was able somehow to survive those events, change my destiny, and choose a path that would bring me happiness and success. I left high school at fifteen years old, got a job, and soon after, found an apartment of my own. I navigated away from a life of uncertainties and volatilities. Luckily, through the nurturing, kindness, and life lessons my aunt and uncle showed me, my confidence soared. They told me I could achieve anything I desired. And I did.

My father was a gritty, hardworking plumber who was truly loved by many. I inherited his personality and the ability to engage and cultivate strong relationships with people. But the best gift he gave me was the drive and the will to succeed, not because he had these qualities but because he did not. He lost everything we had.

My dad had been given a successful plumbing business from my grandfather, but he gambled and drank it away. After that, he managed to lose our beautiful Silvermine, Connecticut, family home. One day, my mom's prized 1966 lemon-yellow Mustang Fastback mysteriously disappeared from our driveway—without explanation, never to return. And I'll never forget the morning—I was probably about ten years old—when throngs of eager tag sale shoppers came into our house and rummaged through each room, leaving with boxes and handfuls of our possessions. Bit by bit, I saw my toys, my clothes, and the contents of my entire bedroom walk out of my home, forever, with strangers. When I repeatedly asked my mom what was happening, she told me to be quiet. I think she was in shock too.

The very next day, we had a terrible ice and snowstorm, but a small box truck still managed to show up and carry away the few belongings we had left. And just like that, suddenly, we lived somewhere else. There was no explanation. Nothing.

Thankfully, my mother had a work ethic like no other, and she showed me that hard work could be fulfilling and rewarding. She, too, lost plenty and dealt with great adversity because of my father; in her mid-forties, she found herself without a dollar in the bank, separated, and nearly homeless. Bruised physically and mentally, she was forced to start her life over paycheck by paycheck. My mother worked as an insurance agent and remained at the same firm for sixty-one years before retiring, staying on through three sets of owners. In addition to her full-time job, she worked weekends as a banquet waitress. Seventy-hour weeks were commonplace for her and also became commonplace for me.

She is super tough and extremely resilient to this day, and I am deeply thankful for her genetic footprint as she continues to thrive at the age of eighty-seven.

My childhood was far from storybook, but I am truly grateful for the lessons it taught me. I am now gritty, resourceful, and extremely independent, and although my past has often caused me great angst, knowing what I know now, I wouldn't trade it for any other life.

Your life defines you, but the future is yours to control. My past made me who I am today: the woman who—over the course of three decades—built one of the most successful and reputable boutique staffing firms in all of Fairfield County, Connecticut.

Through organic growth only, I bootstrapped my business into a $20 million award-winning firm, becoming one of the highest gross profit earners in the industry, and retained a tenured workforce long past those at most other staffing firms. Other staffing businesses coveted my people and practices, day in and day out. And after thirty-one years, I sold my firm in a multimillion-dollar cash deal.

Prior to selling, I ensured that our portfolio of customers was diversified and well balanced; I made sure that no customer made up more than 10 to 12 percent of our total revenue. Additionally, we achieved a gross profit of 45 percent and maintained exceptionally strong and loyal customer relations; most of our customers spanned fifteen-plus years with our firm. Our Net Promoter Score (NPS) averaged 70-plus for both customers and candidates, which was renowned and highly uncommon in the staffing industry. Initially, our firm started in the Connecticut marketplace, focusing on administrative, clerical, and accounting and finance positions in both the consulting and direct-hire verticals. After we grew these two divisions substantially, we expanded into creative, information technology, and medical positions. Additionally, we expanded geographically into the tristate areas and ultimately into several states in the US.

We won numerous awards every year, including first place in "Best Places to Work in Connecticut" and eleventh in "Women-Owned Businesses in Connecticut." Additionally, our business was the leading brand among staffing agencies in the community.

But when our thirty-year anniversary came in 2016, I knew in my gut that it was time to sell. Over the previous two years, I had grown restless within my firm and felt in my heart that I was done with this chapter in my life. My choices were to find investors to grow my firm substantially larger (which would result in many new issues and challenges); grow by acquisition; invest personally; or risk having my perfectly balanced company that I had built become ravaged by a future recession or other business challenges.

I knew the timing was right for change, as staffing firms were being successfully acquired with large multiples, and my company was positioned perfectly for a sale. The staffing industry was due for a major disruption, and the mergers and acquisitions market for staffing firms was at one of the highest levels in fifteen-plus years; there would be no better time to sell.

It's interesting how much clarity and hindsight you gain after you sell your business. Your thoughts are no longer consumed and clouded by the thick of your business. Chaos comes before clarity. Yes, there is confusion at first and some identity issues, but once those fade away, there is a renewed coherence and ability to fully unpack your journey as an entrepreneur and leader. Issues you struggled with so desperately as an owner become obvious in hindsight. You are allowed to go on your journey again but with the complete precision and focus you weren't afforded before.

I decided I needed to share what I've learned along the way: the important lessons of how to guide your business by implementing extraordinary customer service practices, providing exceptional engagement for your customers, using strategic talent optimization practices to hire "best in class" talent, and building a rock-star team of people to share and grow your vision. The lessons I offer aren't things you can learn at Harvard Business School; they are lessons that were learned on the job, by being highly observant, having a willingness to do any job, and seeing the value in delivering unprecedented service to customers. I will teach you how to find someone who might not have the obvious skill set you think you need and show you how to uncover their underlying foundation—revealing a strong structure that can be built on.

Being a successful entrepreneur is exhilarating, but it's not for the faint of heart. Navigating the pitfalls of small entrepreneurial start-ups is no easy task. Eight out of ten small businesses fail in their first eighteen months of operation.[1]

I can help. In my thirty-one-plus years, I have learned a great deal about people and business. Sure, I've made mistakes along the way—none dire, thank goodness! In these pages, I am going to share my top "lessons" with you.

If you don't like constant change, don't thrive in uncertainty, or aren't able to make gut-wrenching decisions quickly, you might want to rethink your decision to run or own your business. Understand that no one will work as hard as you, love your business like you do, or see things quite the way you do. Twelve- to fifteen-hour days become the norm, weekends get cut short, personal and family engagements get sacrificed, and disappointment and frustration are common.

For me, these things were recurring themes, already learned from my childhood. I remember waiting on my aunt's stoop every weekend morning for a mom who often didn't come, and I had plenty of other ugly and upsetting disappointments as a child. However, those moments equipped me with the invaluable tool of resiliency and empowered me to overcome disappointment.

These days, most of us don't get to experience disappointment as often as we should. I believe learning to bounce back from disappointment makes you stronger than ever and gives you new tools for the next time you hit a bump in the road. We need to learn how to fail, how to hurt—and also how to recover and win. Being an entrepreneur offers all of this—the losing, bouncing back, and winning. It's exhilarating, as it allows you to chart your own course, create solutions for customers that you love, help other firms achieve their greatness, build a strong culture filled with like-minded people, and be a part of something thrilling and inspiring. I wouldn't trade my experiences for any other!

Introduction

During my thirty-plus years in the business trenches as a successful entrepreneur, I didn't have the typical higher-learning degrees that often accompany many (but certainly not all) successful business leaders. Along the way, I have succeeded and failed at many challenges, learning from small mistakes and missteps.

I have also enjoyed more than twenty-five years in the remodeling field, restoring old houses, commercial buildings, and condominiums. As I started this book, I couldn't help but continually see the similarities between building and remodeling a physical structure and building a business. When I opened my firm, I was able to clearly see what was needed to build relationships with customers, seeing the end game even before the work began.

Once I set my sights on a customer that I wanted to do business with, I invested my time wisely by finding out everything I could about their company, their products, and their people. I immersed myself in their business; I uncovered their struggles and pain points and then set my sights on helping them. Quite often, their issues were people-related. Therefore, by relentlessly pursuing the customer and showcasing better and stronger talent for them to employ, I developed a trusting relationship with them, and many of their problems went away.

I spent many years working to cut through the distractions and noise of a customer's business to quickly get to the root issues. Whether those issues involved people, marketing, or supply chain problems, I was able to quickly land on the right ideas and solutions and help the customer create better processes. I could do this because I was an unbiased outsider looking in. In fact, I feel fortunate that I was often able to see the result before the journey even began—believing we would be successful even when others didn't. Entrepreneurs often possess the ability to very clearly see their vision even before execution. It's an innate sense that allows them to look far ahead and see the successful outcome even before the venture begins.

This vision carried into the purchase of my first home at the age of twenty-two, when I realized I had the foresight and ability to cut through all the ugliness of a tired home and envision a restored, remodeled one—just as I am able to do when building up a business.

Starting with that very first house, in my mind, I was instantly able to take down walls, move rooms around, reconfigure structures, strip off wallpaper and horrible paint colors, and see a spectacular finished product. And because luck always plays a small factor in someone's success (or because I am great at vetting talent and reading people), I married an extremely talented contractor/entrepreneur. Together, we have taken thirteen structures in disrepair and turned them into profitable turnkey business ventures and homes that we have enjoyed for many years.

The same year I bought my first home and began to build it into my vision, at the age of twenty-two, I also started The McIntyre Group from a blank canvas and grew it into a $20 million business that became one of the strongest, most esteemed staffing firms in the Connecticut marketplace.

My unconventional upbringing and the inability to finish high school taught me the importance of a strong foundation. I realized the importance of it, and I craved it. Starting out with a strong foundation is the key to constructing something solid, whether it is a good business, a building, a relationship, or a marriage. You must be on strong, solid footing when you venture into a business of any kind. From there, you need to create a blueprint, a business plan, or an outline that you will utilize every day to move your business forward. It is critical that you create proper structures, measures, and principles so that everyone has a solid plan to follow. Thankfully, due to the foundation I built my business on some thirty years ago, we were able to withstand three recessions, Y2K, 9/11, and the financial meltdown of 2008–2009—all events that were unplanned and required swift action. If we did not have a solid foundation, we wouldn't have survived.

It all starts with finding the right crew—the group of people whom you hand-select to take your business or project to the next level. Finding, securing, and retaining talented staff is key to your success. Your crew can make or break your business—and your vision—so it's imperative to hire and select the right people. From the beginning, I chose to look for talent that offered diverse views and opinions, which would help grow our firm. I'll admit, my interviewing style was a bit unconventional: I did not demand certain degrees or backgrounds. I sought out strong personality and character traits, like determination, grit, self-awareness, persistence, and a strong moral compass. These are many of the necessary qualities that took me through life and allowed me to grow an extremely successful business; they're traits that no school can teach.

Many of the job opportunities available today don't really need a degree, and firms get too wrapped up in pursuing only degreed candidates. In no way am I knocking people who have degrees—my daughter just finished her master's degree at NYU, and I admire her hard work and achievements. But, so many companies miss out on extremely talented candidates because they don't have a degree, even though they are often far more skilled than the degreed candidate the company chose instead.

I am living proof of this. At the start of my career, I may not have looked like the kind of job candidate who was going to succeed; after all, I had only an eleventh-grade education. But I had other strengths that made up for what I lacked in schooling. I was raised by a woman who showed incredible confidence in me, despite our otherwise bleak family situation, and I took that trust and turned it into a fierce determination to change my life for the better. This, in turn, gave me the drive to excel in sales, which is a very large part of any business—especially the staffing business. My determination to improve my future outpowered any degree I might have earned to become strong in sales and business.

Next is your vision. As a strong leader, you need to articulate your vision for your project or business to those around you, those who might not see your concept from the start. This requires consistent communication, detailed follow-up, and the patience and commitment to continually bring your team back to your blueprints—repeatedly.

Finally, "the devil is in the details." No one will handle the details as you will. No one else will see the small nuances that need to be made to finish setting the stage to make it perfect.

AS YOU READ

This book is broken into seven parts, with twenty key lessons that I learned as a successful entrepreneur, paying special attention to the important things I believe are always worth focusing on. The part titles refer to both the stages of building a business and the stages of building any solid structure.

At the end of each chapter, I will provide key takeaways in the form of a "Punch List": actionable items that you can easily remember, reference, and apply to your business. I promise you, if you put these items into practice and remain consistent, you will build a strong, sustainable business.

Let's grab our shovels and break ground!

PART 1

The Build—Breaking Ground

S o here you are at go time. You've either started a business and need some direction, have that entrepreneurial blood coursing through your veins and want to create your own company, or are looking to buy a firm. In any case, finding or building a good, solid foundation is vital to your firm; a deal breaker would be a foundation that is cracked or crumbling beneath the weight of its framework.

I spent a great deal of time investing in the core structure of my firm, working on its culture, and filling it with top talent. Since I have spent most of my career in the people business, I can tell you that over everything else, people are your most important asset. These days, you can work anywhere, and brick-and-mortar locations are not as important, but your crew—it all boils down to them.

The pressures of owning your own firm are extreme. You'll have to prepare your crew for the ups and downs of the unexpected. By providing the right tools and communicating a consistent and steady vision, you can arm your people for what is lurking around the corners. Most importantly, you must ensure that your crew is one united front, all working together toward the vision you have laid out before them.

Securing the Footings

"You can't build a great building on a weak foundation.
You must have a solid foundation if you're going to have
a strong superstructure."

—GORDON B. HINCKLEY

U nder every house is a foundation, and under most foun-
dations are footings. Footings are an important part of
a foundation's construction. They are typically made of
concrete with rebar reinforcement that has been poured into an
excavated trench. The purpose of footings is to support the foundation and prevent settling. If the footings are not placed properly, or
if the soil conditions were not properly diagnosed, the result could
be problematic, causing weak bearing conditions or outright failure.

If the whole house settles slowly and evenly, some additional settlement is no big deal. But if settlement is uneven

(differential settlement), there could be damage. A frame house with wood siding and drywall interiors can probably handle up to a half-inch of differential foundation movement, but even a quarter-inch of uneven settling is enough to cause cracks in masonry, tile, or plaster.

In construction (and in business), it's the unusual situations that cause the most trouble. When the footing is laid out off-center so the wall misses its bearing, or you encounter a soft zone on site, or the footing is undersized, the builder faces a judgment call. If you think there is a problem ahead, you know you should stop and call an engineer. But if the risk is low, you would like to keep the job moving.

Ultimately, the footings get covered up, thereby burying the problem and removing it from daily visibility. However, if the reinforcement is not done properly, the long-term results can be catastrophic and cause a tremendous amount of damage.

Paving the Way with the Right People

As an entrepreneur, it is critical that you also start with a solid foundation, something on which you can solidly lay the rest of your business. You must continually keep a watchful eye on obvious details that will tell you if you have a foundational issue. Building a strong base is vital to the long-term success of a business, as is doing the right work along the way.

So, what do you need to create a solid foundation? The right people! It starts and ends with finding and retaining the right talent. The company that you build and its culture are important, but the culture is really made by the people. We had people in our company who had outgrown their positions and had no advancement opportunities, but remained with us for an additional two or three years because they loved the people they worked with and the culture we had created.

Let's face it: We spend more time with our colleagues than we do with our own family, so liking who you work with is extremely high-ranking among reasons to stay in your current job. The million-dollar question, and what keeps executives and managers up most nights, is "How do we find the great talent we need to drive our businesses forward?" It starts with the beginning—and the beginning is the interview.

The Candidate: Look Beyond the Résumé

People at my firm often used to question my interviewing style, as I spent a great deal of time asking potential hires about their families and upbringing. I wanted to understand how they were raised and what, if any, obstacles they overcame in their lives. From this information, you can generally understand a person's motivators— why they work, why they do the things they do, what they want out of life, and what decision-making processes they are going to apply to their work. People tend to say they are hardworking and motivated, but it is more important to ascertain this information from their actions, experiences, and background. Your job as the leader is finding out what their principles are, their motivations, and the kind of decision-making skills they would apply to the job. This is vetting and credentialing talent for their behavioral skills.

I remember an extremely competent candidate we interviewed who was raised on a farm. She told me stories of what her days looked like and how, from the age of eight years old, she got up at five a.m. consistently, seven days a week, to start her chores. She told me her family counted on her support and good work to keep the family business moving forward. No task was too menial or beneath her; she did whatever was needed without complaint. What she did *not* have to tell me about was her commitment to hard work. She had grit and determination, and because she shared her personal upbringing with me, I could clearly see how she would apply this strong work ethic to a new job.

This candidate was able to demonstrate that she was not afraid of hard work, was a team player, and would be committed every day. Additionally, she was a great candidate for a start-up operation or small business, as these firms need people who are willing to do whatever it takes to get the job done, with no task too trivial for their job description. She also had a checked ego and required minimal supervision—a superior fit for a small entrepreneurial environment.

My background prepared me for becoming an entrepreneur. I am not saying that everyone must go through what I did, but for me, it helped form who I am and showed me very early that there are a lot of obstacles along the way. Since I was accustomed to emotional volatility, it did not come as a huge surprise when I faced similar issues in business. The unique roller-coaster ride of my childhood—with one side of my family telling me I could do anything I set my mind to, and the other showing me a home filled with erratic, unpredictable situations where I had to be self-reliant—fully prepared me for the roller-coaster ride of being an entrepreneur.

When conducting interviews for your firm, look for what is *not* written in ink, wrapped up in a degree, or readily visible on the résumé. Your focus should include a candidate's behavioral skills, not just their technical skills (i.e., their degrees), especially for roles that might not necessarily require a degree. Many of our customers often got wrapped up in a candidate's degrees and prior jobs and did not take the time to really dig into their background and character. A 2017 Harvard Business School study found that because of degree requirements, three in five employers rejected qualified middle-skill candidates with relevant experience.[1] So take the time to dig into a potential hire's stories, learn about their family and how they were raised, find out what truly makes them tick, and find out why they work. Then you might just hire an exceptional employee.

And keep in mind things are not always as they appear. A candidate was fifteen minutes late for an interview for a sales job opportunity, so the human resources manager crossed him off the hiring list. Thirty minutes later, the candidate arrived soaking wet. He said there had been an accident, so he got out of the Uber in the pouring rain, walked partway, and then ran the rest of the way to get to the interview. This candidate got hired and turned out to be the very best salesperson the company had because he had passion, grit, and determination! You will likely not see these traits jumping off a résumé.

When I meet a young, eager candidate, I think back on the people who took a chance on me—especially in the early days. If you want the best talent, you must find different ways to look for that talent. Stop looking for perfection or trying to check every box. It won't happen and likely will result in you ending up with a less-than-ideal candidate.

In all honesty, I am rather surprised that the résumé or CV has not become a thing of the past. People do not have the bandwidth or the time to sift through résumés all day long. Unfortunately, people put a tremendous amount of painstaking effort into creating a résumé, oftentimes paying several hundred dollars to hire a résumé "expert." There will always be a need for talented recruiters because firms simply cannot afford to take the time to screen through 100-plus résumés to find ten people to interview to fill one opening. On average, each corporate job opening attracts 250 résumés. Of these candidates, four to six will get called for an interview, and only one will get the job.[2] Assuming a company receives 250 résumés for a job opening, and it takes ten minutes to review each résumé, it will take forty-two hours for an individual to screen for one opening!

To maximize time, our firm started by creating bio briefs for our talent, which we then sent to our customers. These briefs summarized our talent's strengths, behavioral insights, and takeaways that were not found on the résumés. By removing the need for our customers to wade through piles of résumés, we returned many hours of precious time back to them.

I would recommend that other companies do the same. Before you start your hiring process, make a list—such as the following—to help you select candidates with the characteristics, skills, and traits you want in your next employee.

- Determine what soft skills (i.e., traits and qualities) you really want in your company. If you have a set of values, think about how those values align with certain attributes, strengths, or skill sets that you want within your company or for a job opportunity.

- Next, create a set of behavioral questions to help you identify these traits in each potential hire. Here are some sample questions you might want to consider asking a potential hire:

1. What are your five best qualities?

2. Tell me a story about one of the following:

   A. Your greatest failure and what you learned

   B. Your most proud moment and why

  c. A defining moment that somehow contributed to who you are today

3. What are your top three strengths? Give an example for each to support those skills as your strongest.

4. What talent or potential do you have that is not fully realized at your current job?

5. What is the most valuable piece of career advice you've been given?

There are many different types of questions you can ask potential candidates to determine their attributes, their depth and commitment, and even their creativity. Asking people personal brand questions about what they value about themselves or asking them to think in metaphors can quickly unlock powerful insights.

1. Which season—spring, summer, fall, or winter—fits your personality best, and why?

2. What would be the title of your autobiography?

3. If you were to choose a well-known axiom or slogan for your life, what would it be? (Bonus points if you can adapt this question for the meeting or job that you are currently interviewing for.)

4. Do you collect anything?

5. If you were a color, which would you be and why?

6. What aspect of your personality adds the most to the world?

7. What is a skill you learned when you were young that
   you still use today?[3]

Questions like these open people up to feeling comfortable and eager to tell stories. The purpose behind this is to create a rapport with the interviewee, allowing them the opportunity to become enveloped in these fond memories, revealing who they really are. If you are hiring someone for a sales or customer-facing role, you will want to hear them tell stories and communicate. By asking these unique questions, you will challenge your interviewee to think about their responses, often producing creative and interesting conversations.

Take the time to create a set of unique and thought-provoking questions that you can discuss with your potential job seekers. I promise you, it will lead to some great conversations and give you some in-depth insights.

The HYMN Method

After I successfully sold my business, I would often go online and read the job postings for C-level executives, vice presidents, and sales managers to see what positions were available. Adhering to what I knew and had counseled for thirty-plus years of my career, I sourced a referral for an extremely adept résumé writer who'd coached a good friend of mine, the president of a large utility company in Connecticut. The writer prepared a masterful résumé for me, which I thought I would use to apply for a position in the corporate world.

However, when I started looking at available job opportunities, I was quickly reminded that my career in the talent acquisition field was far from over and that companies still needed a lot of help managing and creating their talent optimization strategies. It frustrated me to see almost all job openings list mile-long "must-haves," oftentimes including the requirement of multiple degrees. Of course, there are many positions that require degrees, but there are also many that do not!

Ninety-five percent of the time, these job descriptions are about a company's needs and wants but include nothing about the "why" for the person potentially considering them as a place to work.

Firms write a job description but never create a fit and culture description. Take your standard job order requisition, for example, and drill it down to an extremely tight list of absolute "non-negotiables." Next,

When you are writing content for an open position at your company, you want to put yourself in the position of the talent and showcase your company's distinct culture and perks in hopes that their personal brand will match yours, enticing them to apply.

create a list of personality traits that your position needs, what you want in an employee, and who you want representing your brand. Consider the culture of your firm, and factor these attributes in as well. This is an actual job description that I copied from the internet.[4]

SALES MANAGER

What you will do:

Responsible for managing the sales process and driving profitable sales growth within an assigned sales territory to both existing and new customers. You will meet and exceed both corporate and regional objectives for profitable sales growth, A/R management, and customer retention in your territory.

Your responsibilities:

- Develop and execute sales plans utilizing companies' sales directives and guidelines in order to service existing accounts, obtain orders, and establish new accounts. Qualify and pursue sales leads.

- Cultivate customer relationships by developing a deep knowledge of the customer's business and establishing a consultative relationship.

- Engage customers by linking the customer's business priorities to our company's value proposition.

- Prepare sales proposals by quoting pricing, establishing credit terms, and estimated date of delivery to customer based on knowledge of companies' production/delivery schedules and logistics.

- Keep current with industry insights, current company's product mixes, monitor competition by gathering current relevant marketplace intelligence, including information on pricing, products, new products, delivery schedules, and merchandising techniques.

- Partner with internal resources to accomplish growth objectives. Establish and maintain clear and consistent lines of communication with internal departments relative to customer successes, customer opportunities, new customer developments, and other customer-specific information.

- Maintain and submit sales reports (daily call reports, weekly work plans, and monthly and annual territory analyses) as required by District Manager through SAP.

- Actively review and manage existing customer Accounts Receivable balances to help minimize the company's working capital investment and financial risk.

Qualifications Required:

- Four-year college degree

- Four-plus years of direct sales experience in a related field

- Minimum of three years of prior outside business-to-business sales experience to include proven experience and success in solution-selling concepts and a demonstrated history of managing customers throughout a defined sales territory

- Proven success using a consultative sales approach providing multiple layers of value to a customer to establish a mix of sales solutions and products

- Proven success of using their deep knowledge of customer's business, current macro- and microeconomic trends, industry trends, and potential new business opportunities

- Must have excellent organizational, written, and oral communication, listening, and presentation skills

- Self-starter; self-motivated, operates with a sense of urgency; ability to work and succeed independently

- Reliable transportation, current driver's license, minimum liability insurance as required by state of vehicle registration

- Frequent local and regional travel (50–60 percent of work time); minimal overnight travel

- Lives by company's safety programs, OSHA, and all related rules, regulations, procedures, which are applicable to this position's responsibilities

Preferred:

- Familiarity with industrial and specialty gases, industrial gas/welding supply sales

- Working knowledge of SAP

When creating a posting to attract candidates, you must place yourself in the job seeker's shoes—use the perspective of the talent looking for an opportunity. Oftentimes, I call job seeking the "black hole of interviewing" because everything pretty much looks and feels the same. When reading this job posting, ask yourself, "Is this job posting compelling? Do I get excited when I read it? What story does it tell? Would I want to work for this firm? What's their mission, and what is in it for me, the candidate? Is this job worth leaving my job for? Do I align personally with their brand and mission?"

When writing your job posting, use the HYMN method.

- Hook

- Your Why

- Mission

- Non-negotiables

Here is the job posting that I would write for this same position.

HOOK

Are you a natural engager? Would you enjoy representing a brand that brings a safer, more environmentally friendly product to the marketplace? Are you comfortable connecting with new people and eager to listen? Do you like the detective work of researching new customers and opportunities and welcome the challenge of selling a product that benefits both your customers and the planet? Are you hyper-organized and willing to "eat the frog"?

YOUR WHY

Our people work hard, so when it comes time to play, we want you to play hard too! Our unlimited vacation time affords you the opportunity to do just that, and we want you to work wherever you are most comfortable. To keep you in tip-top shape, we offer full medical and dental benefits. Oh, and by the way, there's medical coverage for your furry friends too!

MISSION

Our firm, a leader in the natural gas industry, seeks people like you who will help support and grow our mission of bringing more environmentally friendly products to market. Our BHAG—"Big Hairy Audacious Goal"—is to remove all products except natural gas by the year 2030, ensuring a brighter, better future for all. Since we've grown 30 percent this year already, we need another talented sales expert to help us continue our growth and increase our brand awareness.

NON-NEGOTIABLES

Here are a few requirements we can't live without:

- Two years of sales experience because we want you to understand and appreciate the need for sales expertise in this role. You will be living and performing all things sales-related!

- Travel to our many different facilities about 50 percent of the time, making new friends and visiting exciting locations throughout the US.

- Accountability, commitment, and a teaching mentality; someone who will live and breathe our core values.

- A like-minded person to join us in our mission to build a greener climate and preserve our planet.

Is this a fair comparison? One drab, handpicked job posting versus my well-structured, cherry-picked one? It may not be a perfect comparison, but you get my point. Nothing about that drab job description is memorable. In a candidate job market, most job seekers are screening potential employers by their company culture. Forty-six percent of candidates believe culture is very important in the application process, with a grand total of 88 percent of job seekers citing it as at least of relative importance.[5] When writing a job description, always keep the potential job seeker's view of the opportunity top of mind.

You must start with *why* someone would want to work at your firm and be brief and practical. Do you really need ten years of sales experience, or is this aspirational? Drill down to what is truly important. Creating an engaging dialogue throughout the job posting showcases your brand personality. While you might not have loads of open positions to post, remember you are building a brand. You want people to take notice of your brand, fall in love with it, follow it, and desire to become part of it!

You will have plenty of time to discuss all the duties of the position when you have an actual interview, but the more talent you can engage and hook in the beginning, the better. According to research done by the University of California, the average person on an average day consumes 100,500 words and thirty-four gigabytes.[6] People are being bombarded by email and social media all day long and simply do not have the time, focus, or bandwidth to devote their attention to a long job description filled with your internal jargon. A brief, compelling job posting is best to capture their attention quickly.

Devote Time to Preparation and Engagement

To achieve a successful outcome when meeting and impressing talent for your firm, preparation is needed. In most cases, people don't often prepare for their interviews. It's a mistake to think you are competent enough to wing something as important as an interview with a potential hire. The cost of a bad hire is upward of $15,000 and can be defeating and disruptive to your existing employees, as 74 percent of US companies recently reported.[7] Your people are your most important asset, and the interview, and its process, should be taken very seriously.

Oftentimes, I have seen hiring managers barrel right from a

meeting into an interview in a harried state—completely ill-prepared. In most cases, they repeatedly ask the same questions to the potential hire, which is embarrassing and unproductive. They may also miss key topics that need to be covered or neglect to ask the questions that are needed to vet a strong candidate. This will leave the candidate with a bad impression, discrediting the value of the company's brand and potentially losing them a valuable hire. The last thing you want is a botched interview process, opening the door to the possibility of talent speaking out negatively about the candidate experience or reading prior reviews about other candidates' experiences, as 79 percent of job seekers are likely to use social media as a deciding factor in their job search.[8]

Repeatedly, I ask myself, why do firms go through all the trouble of devoting time and resources to attract good talent, then just completely blow the engagement and interview process? But it happens over and over again. CareerBuilder found that 56 percent of job seekers ranked employer brand as the deciding factor when choosing a new job.[9]

Make sure you block off an hour of uninterrupted time for each interview. Allow fifteen minutes of preparation and résumé review prior to the actual interview and forty-five minutes for the face-to-face meeting. Ask your potential hire the questions you've prepared in advance. If you have a team of people interviewing, let the others ask the traditional interview questions and save the unconventional ones for your interview. But make sure all interviewers compare questions prior to the interview to avoid duplicates. Someone should interview for the behavioral "soft skills," while another manager interviews for the technical "hard skills."

Here are some of the unconventional questions I consistently used when conducting my interviews:

1. Tell me about your childhood and how you were raised.

2. Tell me about your parents. What are their careers?

3. Tell me about your siblings. What are they currently doing?

4. Tell me about the hardest thing you have had to overcome in your life.

5. What did that teach you, or what are your takeaways from that experience?

6. Do you value life experience and respect others' values?

7. When have you failed and what did you learn from it?

8. Tell me something that you have done in your life that you are particularly proud of.

9. Are you creative? What's something creative that you've done?

10. Describe a humbling experience.

11. You seem pretty positive. What types of things bring you down?

12. What was your best day in the last five years?

13. What was your worst?

14. If I asked your best friend to describe you using three words, what would those three words be?

15. If you could do something in business knowing that you would not fail, what would it be?

16. What scares you the most?

17. What are three jobs that you would not take and why?

18. Do you have any pets? (Because I love dogs, and it creates connection.)

These behavioral, "soft skill" questions allowed me to truly get to know the person I was meeting with. It gave me a deep understanding of how they were raised, what made them tick, and how they would fit into a customer's culture. Additionally, it gave me a good baseline on how they would handle the duties and pressures of the role we were recruiting for. It offered insights as to how they would fit in with the other members of the team and how they would work collectively. I was the person who interviewed for the soft skills (i.e., personality traits like leadership, communication, and time management), and our vice president of human resources interviewed for the technical skills (i.e., knowledge, job history, and professional training).

At the start of the interview, I explained to each candidate that I had a rather unconventional interviewing style and that I would not be asking the typical questions most other people asked. I never had a complaint or had someone tell me they were uncomfortable or unhappy, and almost every interview turned into an incredible conversation, which truly allowed me to find out where that person would be happiest and most likely to thrive at work.

By digging deep into someone's upbringing and background, you can get a true sense of what work environment, culture, and management style will best suit them and how they will perform in their job. This process will also help the candidate determine if your firm is the right fit for them because it allows them to be transparent and honest about what they require to thrive and grow. The most important thing you want to unveil is "what is not on the résumé."

Putting the Right People in the Right Seats

Sometimes, however, you find someone who's a perfect fit in every way except one—and that missing piece becomes a deal breaker. This happened in our firm, and we ended up finding a creative solution.

Companies might find that certain groups or types of positions that they hire turn over frequently, causing constant staffing challenges. In my staffing firm, we needed a strong team of recruiting support staff who could handle our extremely robust pipeline of inbound inquiring talent. These roles were ideal for recent college graduates who had two to four years of experience with an interest in the recruiting/human resources space. Our original goal was to hire these individuals, train and develop their skills, and promote them into recruiters, account executives, and business development professionals. Although we did have some success with this, quite often, we lost these employees way earlier in their tenure than we had hoped. In an effort to mitigate this problem, we started having honest conversations with each individual about their career trajectory. One employee joined our firm to potentially take a position in our internal human resources department.

We had open and honest conversations with this person and eventually promoted them into our HR department. But what was most interesting about having these open and honest conversations with our employees was being able to strategize with them about their training, development, and longevity at our company. We were able to take a candid approach with them, knowing they wouldn't remain with our firm forever. We turned it into a training program, had the benefit of having superior talent for a longer-than-expected period of time, and then fully expected them within the two- to three-year period to take a position with another company. Everyone's expectations were met, and we were lucky to enjoy a longer relationship with each employee.

However, there may come a time when you can't find a creative solution to a staffing challenge. Many years ago, we hired an entry-level recruiter to drive the development of new customer relations. He was one of our top five most engaging, positive, and enjoyable employees ever to come to our firm. After months of training, various mentors, and different divisions, he simply could not manage the full-cycle style of recruiting we did at our company. He was an outstanding person and successful account manager, but he could not handle multiple recruitment projects and work with several customers at once; he was a one-trick pony. Because we were a midsized corporate recruiting and staffing firm, we had little distinction in our internal roles. We offered only sales and recruiting opportunities, management opportunities, or support roles.

Ultimately, we had to part ways with this fabulous employee and introduced him to one of our customers for an opportunity they had available. Today, he is the sales manager at a very reputable company. I've watched his progression and seen the favorable reviews people post continually on his LinkedIn page. I'll bet his current employer applauds what a wonderful employee he is every day. This was over ten years ago, and still, not a week goes by that I don't think of this employee with great fondness and a bit of regret that we weren't able to transfer him to a role where he could truly shine. He embraced our values and brought incredible motivation and enthusiasm to our company every day. Sometimes, you just have to let a great hire go.

If someone is not excelling in the position you either hired them for or moved them into, do not get their pink slip ready quite yet; there could be numerous issues causing the setback. First, determine if they are a strong cultural fit for your firm and someone who embraces and upholds the values of your firm. If so, this one is a keeper, and you will want to get to the root of the disconnect. Here are several things to consider:

1. Have they expressed that they are bored? They might feel underutilized and underchallenged, which is easily remedied.

2. They check all the boxes except for one—for example, their sales skills are not strong enough for this particular role. Figure out a way to move them into a different role or somehow modify the position to fit their current skills. You do not want to lose someone like this.

3. They do not fit well in their current team. Ensure that they embrace and fit your values and brand, and if so, attempt to relocate them to another role with different personalities.

4. If you cannot pinpoint the problem, sit down and engage the employee. Let them know that it's okay to speak freely and discuss the position they're currently in and how they feel about it. Let your employee know that you value them as a member of your firm and that you are interested in speaking with them about finding their right seat in your company.

You have taken the time to recruit a talented hire for your firm. Make sure you now take the time to develop, support, and retain them!

⌂ PUNCH LIST

- **Define your "why."** Before you interview prospective hires, drill down on your absolute non-negotiables.

- **Create alignment with HR and management.** Make sure that everyone involved in the hiring process is aligned with the top traits and skills required to hire for this position.

- **Create bio briefs.** Build summaries of talent's strengths, behavioral insights, and takeaways not found on the résumé.

- **Use the HYMN method.** This stands for *Hook, Your Why, Mission, Non-negotiables.*

- **Create behavioral and structural interview questions.** Skip the usual questions and design ones that help determine if the person would be a good cultural fit for your organization.

- **Review, prepare, and time block interviews.** Don't barrel from meeting to interview unprepared and harried. You need clarity and focus to make good decisions.

Prepare for Leadership

"The single biggest way to impact an organization is to focus
on leadership development. There is almost no limit to the
potential of an organization that recruits good people, raises
them up as leaders, and continually develops them."

—JOHN C. MAXWELL

ave you ever heard of collar ties? In construction, collar ties are the tension ties in the upper third of opposing gable rafters and are intended to resist rafter separation in the event of an unbalanced load. Basically, it is part of the support in a roof design and holds things together. A build requires these additional supports in the unlikely event of strong wind uplift or unbalanced roof loads from snow. Taking this concept of support to the workplace, it's time to add some fundamentals and ensure that you have the proper leaders supporting and directing the crew.

You have hired some great talent and are starting to put together a formidable team. As an entrepreneur, watching your dreams come to fruition is thrilling beyond compare. There is nothing more exciting. But you are exhausted, and we are only at mile marker five with a lot more road to cover. How do you get there, and how do you prepare yourself to be the best leader? Let us first recognize and define what a good leader is.

A leader is someone who takes the time to listen intently, someone who can be patient and allow people to feel safe confiding in them. Leaders inspire their people; they show up every day and provide constant and consistent communication. Leaders understand the value of collaboration and hire diversified professionals who appreciate that each team member's contributions are as unique as they are. And finally, leaders need to be courageous, brave, and steady; they need to be prepared to handle difficult tasks. This requires awareness, empathy, and the ability to understand that tough decisions cause a ripple effect throughout the workplace, which needs to be meticulously and caringly managed.

Essential Leadership Tools

BE MINDFUL AND LISTEN

When I started in the corporate world prior to launching my own firm, I was an exceptional listener. I was young, and it was one of the few tools I had in my tool kit—so I used it with great intention and commitment. I was acutely aware of who the successful and respected leaders were at my company. I paid attention to what they did, their behavior during both good and bad times, and how they engaged with people.

In addition to listening, I took copious notes, and I continue to do so to this day. I have boxes and boxes of journals and often refer back to those notes for clarity and insight.

But the reality is, most people are poor listeners. They're generally thinking about what they would like to add to the conversation rather than focusing on what the other person is saying, thus creating a void of lost information. Studies have shown that immediately after listening to a ten-minute oral presentation, the average listener has heard, understood, and retained only 50 percent of what was said. Within forty-eight hours, that drops off another 50 percent to a final level of 25 percent efficiency.[1] You may need to beef up your listening skills, but I promise those skills will help you well beyond the workplace.

BE INSPIRATIONAL

Growing up with my aunt's constant positivity opened me up to the belief that anything is possible. Positive people have more energy and are more self-confident and hopeful. Because of this, they tend to set higher goals and expend more effort to reach those goals. This helps positive people see multiple solutions to problems and make better decisions.

There is also overwhelming evidence from research in positive psychology that people who are happy are more successful. Positivity is related to higher levels of job performance, supervisory evaluations, and perceived customer service. Positive people perform better because they are more motivated and more effective.[2]

It is extremely important for the leader to model positivity, as it is infectious and will likely be mimicked by your staff. If your employees are more positive, results will soar, and your culture will thrive. How can you build positivity?

It starts with recognizing if you are having a tough day or week while acknowledging that things will improve. It's important to reframe your thoughts: Turn the negative into positive. And these tools must be tended to like a house. Perhaps your employees have been working really hard on a long project. Recognize their hard work and give them something to look forward to—like a happy hour or dinner out. Verbal praise also goes a long way—it's vital to give your employees positive recognition through a variety of different ways, such as notes, community praise, gifts, cards, and so on.

I was also a courageous young person, someone who had seen a great deal of uncertainty and disappointment from an early age. It takes courage to create radical change because—let's face it—no one likes to change. People become accustomed to their routines and to their way of thinking. The truth is, it's critical to change—vital, really—because we all need to continue to evolve and grow; without change, we become dormant and stale.

Your job as an entrepreneurial leader is to mitigate as many obstacles as possible by staying ahead of the curve—and ideally, to do this with positivity and good listening.

BE MINDFUL OF DIVERSIFYING

Long ago, we had a manager who thought it best to hire people who were exactly like them. If they had it their way, every person in the company would have matched them exactly. This is a grave mistake on many levels. First, diversity in your firm is critical and something that should be well thought out, with intention and purpose, when hiring; it should be monitored and managed through your human resources department. Additionally, my personal belief is that you should always try to hire people who are smarter than you are and who have diversified points of view.

Having people with different backgrounds, ideals, and beliefs can offer your firm a wider array of ideas and opinions to draw from. When issues and problems occur, you want your firm to be able to respond with diversified viewpoints that can analyze and problem-solve these issues from many angles. When recruiting and retaining talent, 57 percent of employees want to see their company increase diversity, and diverse management boosts revenue by 19 percent.[3]

Having a variety of different personality types really aids in creating a well-balanced environment. In order to achieve a diverse cultural blend in our companies, we should aim to have a combination of personalities: quiet types, creative types, and big personality types.

BE OPEN WITH COMMUNICATION

As a successful entrepreneur, I would advise you to encourage your people to share their ideas and opinions in hopes of creating better processes and growth for your firm. You will be so busy juggling a million different things and putting out fires daily that you will be thrilled to have people who are capable and willing to offer their assistance. You do not want to be the kind of leader who thwarts the ideas of others and only seeks to use their own ideas. This will kill your culture, stall growth, and make your people disengage and seek employment elsewhere.

Oftentimes, people will be reluctant to share their thoughts until they know they are in a safe environment where they will not be chastised. People want to be accepted, heard, and welcomed, so creating this environment is vital to fostering open communication.

It is up to you, as the leader, to ensure that your employees are empowered to speak freely and honestly. Creating a transparent environment goes right back to the beginning stages of hiring. By asking unique behavioral questions, you will create a comfortable dialogue where you can exchange open and honest conversations in your organization.

FOSTER SAFE SPACES

You would not simply walk up to a stranger and share personal, honest information; chances are, that wouldn't be wise—or even safe. Nor would you feel comfortable in a new company voicing your honest and direct thoughts. Again, that often feels unsafe. So how do entrepreneurs and managers create and foster safe spaces so workers feel comfortable sharing their honest opinions and giving authentic feedback?

- **Create talk time.** Allow your employees to have opinions within the walls of your company, and ensure that their opinions are cared for, welcomed, and protected.

- **Share experiences.** Allow your employees to speak openly and honestly, within reasonable boundaries.

- **Create events to build team relations.** Whenever you have the opportunity, break up your existing teams and reassemble new teams so that everyone gets more comfortable and familiar with others in the company. This fosters strong team building, and lifelong friendships are established.

- **Create a buddy system.** It is hard joining a new company. Create a buddy system so each new hire is paired with a longer-term employee. Switch up these partnerships quarterly to continue to acquaint people with one another so everyone can garner different perspectives and share ideas.

- **Be mindful of your responses.** When we ask people for their honest opinions, the way we respond is crucial. If you ask for honest feedback and a team member gives it, don't respond with a defensive rebuttal—even if you're tempted to—or that person will likely never offer their opinion again. As leaders, we must measure our words carefully and ensure that we do not just talk the talk but also walk the walk.

Establish and Communicate Your Company Values and Mission

THE EMPLOYEE HANDBOOK

A good leader has a vision—a plan. To execute that plan effectively and efficiently, you need to create guidelines (a map) to help articulate your strategy. Let us start with an employee handbook. This is a collection of policies, an ever-changing document that spells things out clearly for your employees. People need guidance, direction, and answers to their questions. As a strong leader, you want to make sure your employees are happy and thrive in their new environment. You certainly do not want people getting upset, confused, or bogged down by unclear policies and procedures.

In your employee handbook, start by outlining all of your company policies, including but not limited to

If you do not have clear policies and procedures, your staff will start to create their own.

company hours, key contact information, office and team structures, acceptable protocols, benefits, personal time, social media policies, emergency protocols, and so on. Communicate how you expect your people to function collectively as a company. Consider adding important items like at-will employment (if applicable), an equal opportunity and diversity statement, and a confidentiality agreement. Consider having your employees sign a document stating they have received and read your employee handbook, and place this signed copy in their employee file in human resources.

Much like having a competent architect draft up plans when building or remodeling, it would be best to have an employment attorney or expert human resources firm draft up an employee handbook for your firm. Small businesses that fail to provide their employees with a solid employee handbook risk exposure to potentially crippling compliance and litigation costs. It is critical to be ahead of this rather than behind it. Understand that you need an employee handbook long before you have to actually use it! It is estimated that only one out of four small businesses have an employee handbook.[4] Not only are you helping your employees by laying out what is expected of them, you are also potentially saving your firm from costly litigation.

How you structure your employee handbook is important, as you don't want it to become a list of harsh and negative rules and regulations. By injecting your flavor and tone into your handbook, you can spell out in positive terms your company's policies and procedures, especially if you are a small to midsize firm. Your handbook can be yet another form of branding that advocates for a healthy culture and happy people while spelling out the most critical policies of your company.

Employees need to know what is expected of them, and they want to know what they can expect from the company—it keeps things simple. Ensure you cover all the detailed items at work, including compensation, benefits, sick leave, time off, performance, and many other topics. Having all these topics spelled out in a handbook created by a professional leaves employees feeling confident in their firm and its actions. If you want to be an effective leader, you must provide strong, consistent communication to your people, articulate your message in writing, and repeatedly convey that message to ensure everyone has a full understanding of your vision.

MISSION, VALUES, AND PURPOSE

Next, consider creating what I call MVPs—"mission, values, and purpose"—for your firm. The mission statement is the "what and why" of your company. It provides your company with a clear and effective guide for making decisions, while the values are the fundamental beliefs of the company. Your MVPs define who you are and what you want your firm to accomplish.

MVPs also provide a guiding light and collective goal for your people to aim toward. Small firms need to have their people aligned with the goals of the company. They need their people to be creative, help with operational changes, and assist in creating a healthy culture—even adding the smallest of ideas to benefit the company.

Values show your staff and customers what you truly stand for, what you strive to achieve, and how you hope they will act. They are the fundamental beliefs of the company. For people to do a good job and for managers to lead their people properly and consistently, they need tools and guidelines. Much like the Ten Commandments in religion, your values are the guts of the company: the heart and soul—the makeup of the organization. And remember, character counts. "It's been said that when hiring, employers should trade 90 percent talent for just 10 percent character. Hiring the person who best fits your team is vastly more important than the technical expertise that they may bring."[5] When companies clearly outline their core values, it makes it easier to attract like-minded people who fit in with the company culture, which leads to greater productivity. A company that consistently adheres to its core values also demonstrates integrity, something that can encourage employees to stay even when things get tough.

Creating core values shapes your company culture, creates purpose, and impacts your business strategy. As a leader, it's critical to lay out your vision and provide clear messaging for your people. Ask yourself, "How can I expect to create a great company, create cohesive teams, foster innovation, and have outstanding customer service processes without articulating my mission and values to my employees?" Create a set of values that you are not willing to compromise on. In a recent survey of 1,461 North American CEOs and CFOs, Graham et al. (2017) found that 91 percent of executives view culture as very important at their firms, and 78 percent consider culture as one of the top three to five factors that affect their firms' value. And 50 percent of CEOs and CFOs say corporate culture influences productivity, creativity, profitability, firm value, and growth rates.[6]

There are many ways you can go about creating your values, including hiring a firm to help you. At our firm, we chose to tackle our values internally and went to our management team for assistance. We selected four of our directors to do this, specifically those who truly embodied our company's culture and beliefs and who understood our mission and purpose. We blocked off an entire day and locked ourselves away in our conference room. We gave each director a package of sticky notes, had whiteboards set up in front of the room, and asked them to write down one word on each sticky note that defined who we were, what our firm believed in, and what we stood for. After we had hundreds of stickies on our board, we slowly and intentionally discussed each word and what it meant to our firm. Several hours later, we'd developed a shortlist of words that truly embodied our firm and what we believed in. Our message was both for our customers and for our employees.

To be certain, we reconvened in a week to review our work. After a final review and a few tweaks, I worked with one of our creative leaders to build short statements that complemented our already established brand. As part of our marketing strategy, we used quotes from leaders like Steve Jobs, Oprah Winfrey, and Walt Disney to enhance our values and their meanings. This was one of our most successful projects; everyone felt strongly about our work and the values on which we had decided, matching our already positive and strong culture. In fact, almost half—46 percent—of job seekers cite company culture as very important when choosing to apply to a company.[7]

STAY TRUE TO YOUR VALUES

Creating a set of catchy values and not living by them could prove to be a very poor decision. Being a good entrepreneurial leader means consistently communicating and reiterating your message and vision. Your values must be taken very seriously.

Values cannot be aspirational.

Of those firms that have values, I would say only about 25 to 30 percent know what those values are, follow them consistently, or even take them seriously.

If you are not committed to holding every person in your firm accountable to your values repeatedly, do not create them, as you will do more harm than good. You must create a set of values that you expect everyone in the company to follow, 100 percent of the time, without fail or exception. The management team must embrace these values as consistently as you, the leader, do, or you should go back to the drawing board and reconsider your approach.

A friend of mine who is president of his firm had a very talented sales manager who had been at his company for more than twenty-two years. The company had a set of values it followed—*most* of the time. A situation occurred whereby the sales manager changed some important data on a shared spreadsheet that all the salespeople followed, ultimately changing some of the commissions for one of the salespeople on his team. When the sales manager was asked if he'd changed the spreadsheet, he vehemently denied it. But the president had the ability to check the software to see who, in fact, made the edits, and he discovered that it was indeed the sales manager. Word spread quickly, and everyone ultimately found out that it was the sales manager who had intentionally tried to sabotage one of his own employees.

From the outside looking in, I'm certain you're thinking that it would be an obvious, easy decision to terminate the sales manager immediately. When you are on the outside of a decision, one that's not yours to make, seeing what needs to be done is often very simple and "emotionless." However, in this case, the sales manager was a very dear friend of the president's, had been with the firm for twenty-two years, and was an excellent producer. The president was beside himself. He lost several days of sleep over this issue and turned to the members of our executive forum group for guidance. What might seem obvious to us was instead a gut-wrenching decision for him, for the financial health of the company, and for his friendship with the salesman.

One of their company values was "Act with integrity and honesty at all times." Had he not terminated the sales manager, the president would have lost all credibility throughout the entire firm, and the employees would have never again paid attention to those values. Instead, he used the company values as part of the dialogue and reinforced this message after terminating the sales manager. By doing so, he provided strong reassurances and sent a clear message to his people, showing his staff that he truly was a leader who stood by the company's values and expected the employees to follow those values. Leaders must be true to their values at all times, not just when it is convenient for them; otherwise, there is no accountability demonstrated to their employees.

Some firms do not start with an MVP. Whatever the reasons might be, they institute their MVPs down the road. Oftentimes, a start-up operation has little to no staff and must prioritize launching the business and generating revenue before it starts conceptualizing itself with branding and structure. It also can take time to identify who you, the company, truly are. The most important part of your MVPs is getting full support and adoption from your management team and making sure those values are shared and believed in throughout the company.

One thing you cannot do is come up with your MVPs, post them in a few places, and hardly make mention of them again. Your MVPs must become a part of your daily dialogue, mentioned and used in each meeting, reiterated in one-on-one meetings, and used in discussions with your employees—perhaps even in their reviews. Your MVPs function as the foundation of your firm.

PUTTING OUR MVPS INTO PRACTICE

When our firm created our MVPs, we started with a fun contest to introduce our employees to our values and ensure they remembered them and understood their importance. We printed some cool pins that had key words on them, like *Bold, Hustle, Crush It, Resourceful, People over Profit, Customer Obsessed.* We asked our employees to nominate their colleagues when they saw someone carrying out one of our values in a positive and unique way. In our monthly town hall meetings, I would praise the employees who nominated other employees they saw demonstrating our core values. We did this for about a year, which helped reinforce the values and showed a consistent effort to keep them top of mind.

At our summer picnic, we had a contest where teams of employees had to take our company values and turn them into a song or rap. This fostered team building and helped our employees remember and live by our values. (Plus, it was great video content for future use!) Once this program ended, we started adding interview questions that mirrored our values and retooled our interviews to ensure potential hires fit into our culture. We also chose to incorporate our values into our annual employee reviews. This made it much easier to create alignment and to speak with people when they were not following our mission, values, or purpose.

Preparing for leadership starts with hiring the right people, fostering open and honest communication, and being visible and present. Next, provide your people with the proper tools, direction, and road map so that they can easily understand and execute your vision. Your job is to make sure you continually hire the right people, nurture them, and feed them with knowledge and training so that they can flourish within your organization. If you continually challenge your people, allow them to learn, give them a voice and a seat at the table, and provide them with open and honest direction, they won't have a reason to look elsewhere for work.

◻ PUNCH LIST

- -

- **Develop a branded handbook.** This is the first thing you give your new employees. It should be thorough and updated regularly.

- **Create your MVPs.** Decide on your mission, values, and purpose.

- **Establish your "why."** And be sure you communicate it to your employees.

- **Hire for diversity.** Look for diversified hires that offer alternative perspectives different from your own.

- **Create safe spaces.** People work better when they're valued and feel secure, not when they're constantly looking over their shoulder or worrying.

- **Communicate and reiterate.** Live and breathe your MVPs in the daily running of your company.

Build Your Bench

"Great vision without great people is irrelevant. If I were
running a company today, I would have one priority above all
others: to acquire as many of the best people that I could. The
single biggest constraint on the success of organizations today is
the ability to get and hang on to enough of the right people."

—JIM COLLINS

In the building industry, a general contractor hires a variety
of different vendors that specialize in electrical, plumbing,
HVAC, tile, and such. These vendors are critical to the contractor's business and are the lifelines they come to depend on. General
contractors evaluate each vendor, continually checking their work
for a high level of performance, quality, timeliness, efficiency, and
so on because their work defines the contractor's work and reputation. Those that do not perform at a high level get removed

from the vendor list, and the contractor hires replacements. All elite general contractors continually upgrade, reevaluate, manage, and strive to improve what they have in order to build the best team possible and maintain a stellar reputation.

If they cannot grow and excel with their current vendors, they replace them—no emotion, no fear—because general contractors have one common goal: to win more business! If you look at successful businesses, they will undoubtedly have an exceptional leader whom they trust and follow and a very cohesive group of exceptional people who work together toward one common goal. As an entrepreneur and strong leader, you must invest consistently in finding great people to fill your bench.

Let us get to the real root of this issue: Why do firms tolerate bad behavior and often keep employees who are mediocre performers or a poor fit for the company? Face it: If you had a crew of A-players just waiting to join your firm, you would send your ill-fitting, culturally imbalanced personnel packing this afternoon—wouldn't you? Yet companies don't do this because they do not have an adequate pipeline of talent.

Companies only focus on their immediate needs. They only focus on the fires that are currently burning, not on those fires that will come up in the future. Few firms are building a pipeline of future talent; instead, they continually invest in upgrading their mediocre talent. When a resignation comes in, everybody panics and scrambles because the pipeline doesn't have replacements lined up. This shouldn't be the case, and I'm going to talk about how to change that. No one should have their back against the wall when hiring talent!

The Talent Pipeline

Why is it most firms have a strong sales process yet no process for the recruitment of talent for their firm? You should have a sales pipeline and a talent pipeline—it's that simple. Creating a strong process for pipelining talent requires an investment of time and money. Don't be one of those companies who post a job opening (often after the resigned candidate has left the company) and rush to find someone to fill the vacancy. Posting and praying is not exactly a consistent, well-thought-out hiring strategy!

In my experience, about 70 percent of firms don't have proper job descriptions for their positions, have not drilled down on what they really need—only what they *think* they need—and management has not finalized candidate requirements. Fewer than 20 percent of firms that I have spoken to over the years have a documented process outlining their interviewing procedures.

A tremendous amount of time and money is wasted on advertising, interviewing, and managing this large and cumbersome hiring process, only to garner one hire. Let me remind you that your firm is being interviewed and vetted by the candidate just as much as the candidate is being interviewed and vetted by you. With all the choices and job opportunities today, you must be extremely cognitive of the first impression you make on a potential job seeker. As they say, you get only one chance to make a first impression.

As I mentioned in Lesson 1, most managers run into their interviews harried and ill-prepared, without an agenda, asking the same questions the last two managers asked. And then, once a candidate is selected and hired, the remaining candidates' résumés get tossed into a filing cabinet, never to be looked at again. None of this talent is preserved for future opportunities. Thank you calls and follow-up calls are not conducted, and the company returns to business as usual. What a waste!

THE ALPHABET EXERCISE

Let us first look internally at your current employees. You most likely can bucket your internal employees into a combination of A, B, C, and D-level talent, with A being your best performing, most motivated, and most valuable employees, and D being your least talented, least specialized, and most easily replaced workers. Since your greatest investment is your people, you should constantly be looking to upgrade your internal talent. Not only will the company demand it as you grow, it is the single most important and smartest thing you should be doing in your company. It's actually more important than driving sales and servicing your customers because those important activities will naturally follow if you have top talent at the helm.

It's not about putting more boats in the ocean; it's about getting the right boats in the ocean!

If you develop your staff to A and B players only, you will likely spend less time worrying about customer engagement and securing business, as these kinds of "best in class" employees will innately get it!

Here is a simple exercise to help you accurately grade and define your existing employees while removing the emotional ties that prevent us from making the right decisions. I call it my Alphabet Exercise.

First, gather your key leaders together and draft out a grid on a piece of paper or whiteboard. Now create the criteria that makes the A and B Players:

1. Meet or exceed goals

2. Act as a role model for all employees

3. Exceed customers' expectations

4. Fit our firm's culture

5. Do whatever it takes to move the company forward

Write out these criteria in a row at the top of the grid. If you have values that are appropriate for this exercise, I recommend you use them instead of my examples.

Now, take each of your employees and place their names in a column on the left of the grid. Give each employee a letter ranking under the criteria you listed.

USE YOUR MVPS (MISSION—VALUE—PURPOSE)

Employees	Goals	Role Model	Culture Fit	Team Player	Adheres to Policies
Bob Jones	A	C	B	C	D
Paul Jaffe	B	A	A	A	B
Neera Burke	A	B	A	B	A
Alberto Puck	B	B	B	B	A
Susan Smith	B	C	D	C	C

A = Exceeds Target   B = Meets Target   C = Under Target   D = Below Target

The A category, or grade, exceeds the target or goal; B category meets the target or goal; C category is under the target; and D category is way below expectations or failing.

When you conduct a whiteboard exercise like this, it removes the emotion and allows you to focus on the results. If you are conducting this exercise as a team of high-level executives or managers, have each leader put the grade on a sticky note and walk it up to the board. Each of your grades should be very close to one another's; if they're not, you will need to have a conversation about the employee in question.

The employees that I highlighted in the box—Bob Jones and Susan Smith—should be replaced without exception. Additionally, if there are people like Bob who are high performers but negative promoters of culture and policy conformance, you need to make some gut-wrenching decisions. Our goal is to have only A and B players in our companies. Yes, you might be forced to let go of some workers who have been there a while or gotten quite comfortable in their roles, but the result—only A and B players—will be worth it.

I remember a time at our firm when we had a superior sales manager. He was incredibly talented and made several million dollars a year for our firm. Every year he exceeded his sales goals and always achieved his bonuses for higher-than-expected revenue. Every marker we put out for him he successfully met or exceeded. However, he was not culturally aligned to our values or policies, and over a period of time, he became difficult to deal with, especially when working within our teams. A large part of his role was to interact with recruitment teams; he counted on their efforts. Unfortunately, he would often pressure his colleagues when they didn't do what he asked or couldn't find a candidate fast enough for a sales requisition that he brought in.

We went through the proper channels and had meetings and wrote him up several times, but he refused to change his behavior. He had no accountability for his actions and was solely focused on the numbers—to the point that he felt nothing else mattered. There

CREATE A SUCCESSFUL PIPELINE

Let's tackle all the other strategies and methods you need to implement a successful candidate pipeline—one that will continually feed all your recruitment needs and create future hires down the road. To maximize your efficiency when hiring, you need to engage candidates in a seamless manner, ideally using **no more than ten touches of communication per candidate** before getting them into your funnel. By "touches," I mean emails, phone calls, even in-person meetings with potential hires. If potential hires find your hiring process to be arduous, they will simply quit the process of applying altogether.

Determine how you can streamline your application process so that the whole thing (excluding the interview) takes less than five minutes. Test the process out yourself and make sure you find it easy and efficient. Is the application easy to fill out? Does it require unique software, or can anybody with internet access fill it out easily and quickly? Don't make it complicated, and don't make it too technical.

Have you ever gone online to order something and become so frustrated that you actually left the site of the product and went to find it on Amazon? I have done that more times than I can count! Why? Because Amazon takes just two clicks to buy things. It is seamless, efficient, and easy. This is the experience needed to garner exceptional talent! Save the details and extensive vetting for the actual face-to-face interview. Applicants have busy lives; respect their time. You want to attract them, not turn them away. Sixty percent—well over half—of all job seekers report quitting in the middle of filling out online job applications because of the length or complexity of the automated process.[4]

Today, we must be acutely aware of those who are searching for their next great job opportunity! Immerse yourself in their operating reality and experience the entire process from their point of view. This will help you quickly remedy any poorly created processes or technical snags and ensure a seamless, enjoyable, engaging experience for your potential hires.

⌂ PUNCH LIST

- **Always be recruiting.** You want a talent pipeline you can call on in the future.

- **Apply the alphabet.** Use the "A, B, C, D" method, with "A" being a great fit and "D" being the worst. Do this for your staff quarterly.

- **Apply the wand mentality.** Ask the "magic wand" question: If you could wave a magic wand and wish away any employee without repercussions, who would it be? Again, do this quarterly.

- **Build for the greater good.** Do not prioritize the benefit of just one (subpar) individual.

- **Use ten touches or less.** Create an application process that is nimble and fast or risk losing top talent.

Envision the Journey

"Give ordinary people the right tools, and they will design
and build the most extraordinary things."

—NEIL GERSHENFELD

When you interview general contractors or builders for a potential job, you do not ask them if they have tools. You assume they have the proper means to perform their jobs for you. However, you definitely need to screen them for other qualities. What is their work process? Is their personality a good fit for you? What about their reputation and completed projects?

Companies hire corporate recruiting and staffing firms because they are the experts in finding passive talent (people who are not really looking to change jobs). Staffing firms attract, recruit, and deliver some of the best passive talent to customers, and they cultivate strong relationships with talent that might not be quite ready to enter the job market yet.

Pipelining talent requires the work of a devoted team, following a systematic process, consistently managed over a long period of time. It also involves sourcing, speaking to, and meeting large quantities of people repeatedly to extract only one perfect candidate for a job opportunity. Often it feels like a game of numbers, but it's a refined game, and a well-oiled machine makes it look easy.

Some companies don't have the capacity or the time to set up this kind of systematic process to attract and engage talent. Others do not understand or appreciate the value that this talent optimization model can bring to their companies. This is a missed opportunity.

Much like home renovations, most people have little interest in designing their own renovation process, let alone the ability to envision what's possible. This is why you will find so many remarkable engineers, home stagers, home builders, architects, and designers in the industry. A competent designer can cut through the clutter and ugliness of something and see the vision of a completed renovation. They see things that most do not and enjoy the challenge of turning a dated mess into a gleaming new showpiece. They also can extract from the buyers exactly what their vision is and what they want their finished project to look like. Like all industry experts, they have tools and products that help them do their jobs more efficiently and bring their thoughts and sketches—including blueprints—to life.

You must have a blueprint for hiring so that you can fill your company with strong leaders who can drive and grow your business.

Likewise, when it comes to hiring, every company needs a blueprint, a plan that can be easily followed, tweaked where needed, and passed along to new team members when that time comes.

In prior lessons, I offered a strategy for hiring correctly by making your own non-negotiables list. You can build your blueprint for job requisitions by following the HYMN method (hook, your "why," mission, non-negotiables). In conjunction with HYMN, create an interviewing organizational chart outlining who does what in the hiring process, and be sure everyone follows it. A consistent process for hiring can be replicated again and again regardless of turnover within your hiring team.

I've previously suggested a timeline for hiring to ensure that you do not lose any potential hires. Now I want to address how you can extend a rapid-fire job offer, create a streamlined process for credentialing, and manage the onboarding process. Nothing is worse than witnessing companies go through the work to attract, find, and engage top-tier talent, only to then lose this talent because of a long and drawn-out paperwork process.

The Application Experience

Your application experience is the candidate's first peek into your company. Presumably, they have already googled your firm, gone to your website and reviewed your team's page, and perhaps even investigated the people and culture your firm already has in place, looking for the right culture fit for themselves. If you have a poor or incomplete social footprint, they likely would have already voluntarily ended the application process.

But let's assume they want to move forward. They must become familiar with whatever platform or application channel you use to screen your inbound candidates. This is where you must engage your potential candidates in ten or fewer touches; otherwise, they will likely become frustrated and end their application process with you. Remember, this is not a prescreen or an interview; this is merely to get potential candidates into your pipeline quickly so that you can immediately elevate them to the interview stage. If you choose to use an outsourced job board or application, make sure speed and efficiency are tops on the list!

In prior lessons, we discussed creating a streamlined interview process to ensure that your candidates remain engaged, interested, and available for your potential job opportunities. Now you need to remain steadfast and focused on getting the candidate to the finish line.

Presenting the Offer

A company can really bungle the candidate experience by not operating efficiently when extending an offer to a potential candidate. Some firms can take weeks to prepare and send an offer letter to a potential new hire.

This is completely unacceptable! Think about this through the eyes of the enthusiastically expecting candidate. Not only are they left in the dark wondering what is going on, they are also experiencing great angst and anticipation waiting for you to call or email with your decision.

Your company should have a readily available draft of an offer letter where you can simply plug in the salary and job title. From the moment you and your management team decide this is the candidate you want to extend an offer to, extending the offer should take no more than seventy-two hours. Make sure you have a project leader managing this process, and be sure that no one drops the ball!

Reference and Background Checks

Reference checks and background checks are options for your company to consider. You must be consistent in whatever policies and procedures you create around references and background checks and ensure that a high level of confidentiality is used when gathering this information. Additionally, the prospective hire must sign a release to permit reference checks and allow you to gather the necessary information to run a background check. I strongly recommend that you work with a reputable and licensed background check provider who can guide you through this process.

We performed lengthy reference checks on behalf of our customers. However, one question—asked of the candidate's former employer—seemed to provide me with the only answer I needed: "Is this candidate eligible for rehire at your firm?" Whatever the answer, it gave me the clarity I needed to make a confident decision.

I strongly recommend that you conduct your reference and background checks in a timely and efficient manner, as "time kills all deals." Nothing is worse than going through the extensive and time-consuming process of finding the ideal candidate only to lose them to a competing offer because of slow paperwork or unnecessary procedures.

Don't Underestimate Onboarding

The acquisition process does not stop once you send the offer letter; it's actually the start of your ongoing candidate experience. I can't tell you how many times we got a call that a new hire was left in a customer's lobby unattended for hours on their first day. After all that work to recruit, interview, and hire the candidate! There is no excuse for this, and it must never happen. In fact, the quality of the onboarding matters. A recent study found that 33 percent of new hires leave their new company before ninety days due to poor onboarding! Beyond that, a whopping two-thirds, or 69 percent, of employees say they're more likely to stay with a company for three years if they experienced greater onboarding, and 58 percent of them are more likely to stay with the organization after the three-year point if they received structured onboarding.[2] It is vital to have an extensive onboarding process to welcome your new hire to your company.

THE FIRST TWO WEEKS

Here is what your onboarding packet and agenda for the first two weeks should look like:

- Receipt of onboarding documents: complete confidentiality/noncompete paperwork if applicable; nondiscrimination pledge; tax forms; and identification documents

- Receipt of company policies: review employee handbook, dress attire, benefits, PTO, eligibility, and so on

- Discussion of security: assign card-key or badge, issue laptop, review technology protocols, and so on

- Discussion of payroll, forms, reimbursements, and so on

- Discussion of culture and MVPs (mission, values, purpose)

- Questions and additional information

Our human resources manager would block off the entire morning to review and fully onboard all new hires. Once this process was finished, she would bring the new hire around our office, introduce them to each employee, and transition the new hire to the next person responsible. This person then took our new hire out to lunch and was assigned as their mentor for a two-week period, much like a buddy system. The new hire then followed a two-week agenda, which never allowed for a lag in training or left them alone without a person they could consult with.

THE WELCOME BASKET

When a new hire finally got to their desk, they were greeted by a welcome basket full of company swag, a greeting on their computer screen, and an office area fully stocked with supplies. Our IT department had also already completed their email and desk setup and needed to sit with them for only a few moments to review their passwords and protocols.

GETTING TO KNOW YOU

At the end of the first day, each new hire was sent a questionnaire of "fun facts" about them, which they filled out and sent back to our marketing team. Our marketing team then created a photo of the new hire along with this information, reintroducing our new hire to everyone at the company.

Creating Engagement

I suggest implementing two check-in meetings for your new hires: at thirty days and at ninety days. You need to ensure your new hire is acclimating happily. This is also a way for you to mitigate any potential problems that might crop up early on. Prepare an outline of questions you will be asking to ensure you cover everything you want to discuss. These meetings are extremely valuable for both you and your new hires.

Consider any other areas in your firm that might potentially cause confusion to a new hire. If you have other locations, consider creating a visual directory using LinkedIn images or company photos, with the employees' contact information, title, seating information, and travel itineraries, if applicable. By including travel itineraries, you are able to easily know that person's calendar and whether they are available or out of the office.

By implementing these tools and processes, you will help your new hires navigate their new environment and achieve higher productivity in a shorter time frame. Remember that the cost of one bad hire is upward of $15,000, so you want to prevent as many pitfalls as possible and hire the right people, the right way, the first time.[3]

⌂ PUNCH LIST

- **Create a candidate pipeline.** Companies benefit from having a pipeline of qualified talent. If you can't keep this going, hire a firm to help.

- **Remember that time kills all deals.** Be prompt, pay attention, and don't waste people's time.

- **Act fast and have a plan.** Have an offer and action plan ready when you offer the job to your new hire.

- **Own your onboarding.** Be consistent across departments.

- **Always be cultivating.** Continue to cultivate culture, and you will continue to cultivate your employees.

PART 2

Draft an Award-Winning Plan

As with any good strategy, start with a list of wants and needs. When buying real estate, this is called a "deal breaker" list. You may not get everything on the list, but you need to ensure that you have a prioritized list and a game plan. You also need to know what your absolute non-negotiable deal breakers are.

You've no doubt heard the old real estate joke: What are the three most important things to look for when buying a house? Answer: Location, location, location. Sure, you can renovate, remodel, or even remove a home, but you cannot move its location or change its neighborhood.

Likewise, you need a singular focus when hiring talent; you want the best. Much as you may seek to live in a wonderful community and neighborhood, you want to surround yourself with incredible "best in class" talent. Once you start to build and grow your employee community, you will find that like-minded people enjoy spending time with similar folk. This strengthens your culture and increases your chances of recruiting more people like the ones you already have!

Remember, training and development will enhance a talented employee, but the foundation must be solid and match your hiring initiatives and culture.

Construct the Frame

A team is a group of people with different abilities, talents,
experience, and backgrounds who have come together for
a shared purpose. Despite their individual differences, that
common goal provides the thread that defines them as a team.

—WISDOM IN THE OFFICE

The footings are placed, the foundation has been laid,
and now the framing begins! You are ready to build the
structure. To build the right structure, you need to follow a detailed set of blueprints. Blueprints give you the necessary
instruction to get to a solid final project. For a structure to come
out accurately, you need a plan, and you must rigorously follow it.

Everyone works best when you have an MVP (mission, values,
purpose), along with a strategic game plan to follow. Builders follow their blueprints, but what plan do you follow to keep the most

important assets of your firm in place and excited about working at your company?

For a company to build a successful talent pipeline, it must create a model to recruit talent. But this is not merely the creation of a good process to find talent—it goes way beyond that. You cannot rely on just one source, like job fairs, for all your recruiting needs. You must invest in multiple verticals that are consistent and structured.

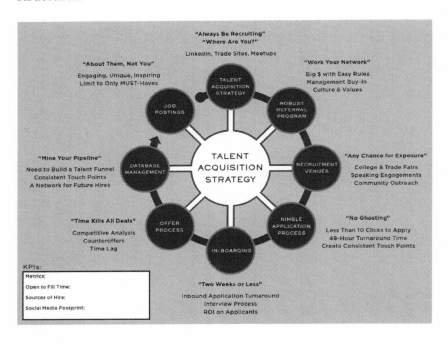

Your management team must be acutely aware that sourcing, engaging, interviewing, and hiring "best in class" talent requires focus and commitment in all stages of the recruitment process. While you might be fortunate enough to have attracted a stellar candidate, if you stall on their application, interview, or offer process, you will likely lose them or create a disenchanted candidate who will move on to another firm.

Without a predetermined and structured process from the first point of engagement with a potential hire, through the full cycle of interviews, to the actual start date, the recruitment process could potentially fall apart. Additionally, you are causing damage to your social footprint and to your reputation. Over time your reputation in the marketplace will continue to decline, and you will likely attract fewer and fewer candidates. Word spreads, and reviews matter. In fact, a whopping 74 percent of job seekers read at least four reviews before forming an opinion about a company.[1]

The Many Roads to Recruitment

For a company to build a successful talent pipeline, it must set up and maintain a variety of diverse processes. When one avenue of recruiting does not work, another could flourish. Keep your eyes open for new ways to tap into talent.

To keep the talent pipeline flowing, you must be able to pull from a variety of verticals.

Do not count on just one area of recruitment to supply you with the talent you need; you must utilize a model like the one I gave earlier. This requires an invested talent acquisition team and a structured process the team can follow. The reason staffing firms find talent so quickly and efficiently is because of their investment in these verticals, their pipeline-management consistency, their database development, and their committed development process. Companies must build the exact same process for these many reasons.

Establish what is mandatory for your operational success and what is not. Define a recruitment strategy that is best for your firm. Start by looking at all your past employee hires, both successful and unsuccessful. Where did they come from, and what has made them successful? Did they come from your industry? A competitor?

Same background and culture? Have successful hires come from any industry or industries that are similar? Put together a list of past-hire "common denominators." Gather statistical information that will be useful to your future hiring patterns.

One time when we hit a roadblock at our firm and found that we weren't hiring the right candidate profiles, we decided to review all our existing and most successful hires (our As and Bs) and dig deep into their employment backgrounds and personal history to find the common denominators. This wasn't as difficult as it may sound. Once we found these common threads, we started building profiles and recruiting for these similar backgrounds. There might be some things you're willing to be flexible on, but you'll want to stand firm on your non-negotiables.

The Brag Behind the Brand

Next, create a killer internal referral program. Giving large dollar bonuses to your internal employees is a whole lot better than giving it to outside resources. We invested deeply in our internal referral program; when employees brought us candidates whom we ended up hiring, we rewarded those employees. Then, when we realized we needed to double down and expand on this program, we engaged the management team and discussed the program at every opportunity.

This program became a daily conversation with our people. We brought it to our town halls, infused it into our culture, and discussed it in quarterly meetings, director meetings, and several times a month with each member of our firm. You will find that the most successful hires at your firm tend to spend their time with like-minded people. If you don't have a people program to attract internal referrals at your firm, create one now!

Mike Stafiej, CEO of ERIN—an app that supports employee referrals, bonuses, and so on—has discovered the financial rewards of these referrals. He claims that "$7,500 per hired employee referral is the amount saved in productivity and sourcing costs. Forty-five percent of employees sourced from employee referrals stay for longer than four years, and only 25 percent of employees sourced through job boards stay for over two years."[2] When you invest in your people and their personal interests, you are creating a culture that they want to brag about.

I have found that young people enjoy showcasing their accomplishments by way of social media, through friend groups, and through conversations with their peers. Whereas I, as a fifty-six-year-old, would ask someone, "What do you do?" a younger person would ask, "Where do you work?" Take this opportunity to build bragging points for your employees—"the brag behind the brand."

LIVING YOUR BRAND

Young people literally look at their company as though it is a part of their identity. They infuse it into every facet of their life. They can't, nor do they want to, be tethered to their desks seventy hours a week, and this is a way for them to showcase their services and beliefs in a modern way. Whereas older people may have a "grind it out" mentality, younger people remain extremely passionate and connected if they are invested in their brand.

Have you ever heard of a digital media company called "Barstool"? (Disclaimer: this is a young and racy brand.) This is a company that has a phenomenal social media presence and is highly sought after by young people for career opportunities. They have taken their brand and customer engagement to unprecedented levels and are the epitome of the "work hard, play hard" mentality for the next generation. Everyone wants to work there! Chick-fil-A, WeWork, Chobani, and Zappos are also excellent examples of brands that use their social media to engage and bolster their employee following.

This completely supports my point about living a brand. It's extremely important that you can relate to *all* of your employees and that you try to see all aspects of your company through the eyes of your people. Take time to find out what really would inspire your people to give referrals. Perhaps instead of money, consider matching a 5k sponsorship for one of your employees' favorite charities. This is a home run on so many levels, as it supports health and wellness, supports a needed charity, creates exposure for your firm, and gives your employees the opportunity for bragging rights and additional social media exposure. If you have multiple offices, you could make it a team contest, challenging each location to raise the most money for the charity.

BRAGGING ON YOUR BEHALF

Remember, although you need to make a consistent effort to inspire your people to give referrals, the reward doesn't have to stay the same. If you believe your people would like the reward to change, then change it; otherwise, set an amount that is really going to motivate someone, and be consistent in reminding your staff of the importance of assisting with the recruiting efforts.

If you are struggling to determine the monetary value of a referral or the structure of your program, ask around and find out what like-minded firms are doing. If the cost of a bad hire is approximately $15,000, consider what it is worth to you to have a successful hire. There is no right or wrong answer, but a strong referral reward in the neighborhood of $2,500 will likely get people excited and inspired to work hard on the company's behalf. Speak to your teams often about their friends and business colleagues. If your employees are happy in their job, they will be very excited to find people to come work with them! The greatest benefit of all is that you get vetted, reliable referrals, as no one will recommend a slacker or bad employee to a firm that they love!

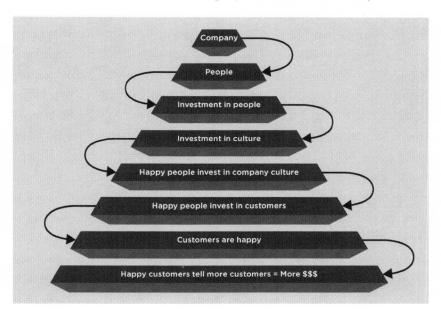

I can tell you from experience, your program needs to be simple and consist of few rules and very little (or no) red tape. Make sure you vet out any program and work out the kinks before you roll it out to your people! Nothing is more discouraging than a program that has a million hoops to jump through or small print to navigate. Be concise when spelling out your referral program, and create an easy process with no more than a few steps. Make sure your accounting department understands the importance of this program and ensures timely payment to those referring people to your firm. Nothing will make the program fall apart quicker than your own employees having to chase down their referral checks! It is easy to take a well-intended program and have it sink down the drain.

On the other hand, if you have not built a strong culture and a solid foundation, it will be very difficult to create buy-in for a successful referral program. Unhappy employees will talk about their company as much as happy employees will, so it is imperative to build a strong culture. Even if you offer $10,000 for every referral, if people are not happy where they work or cannot get behind the brand, they won't refer people (especially friends) to your company. It is extremely important to work on the fundamentals first—for example, the foundation and structure of your company—and then work on the other elements of the talent acquisition model.

How you respond to the referrals you receive from your people is of great importance to your reputation. The candidate experience and process of managing personal referrals must be given white-glove treatment. I believe that all candidate management should be done this way, but it is critical that you offer these referrals a timely, professional, engaging experience. Having an expeditious application process, a fast turnaround time for interviewing, a smooth and organized interview process, and detailed, consistent follow-up will be extremely important to the employee who referred the candidate. Embarrass them in any way, and consider your referral program over!

Many Roads to Recruitment

When you start building out your own talent acquisition model, consider all of the possible avenues available to you: trade shows, job fairs, job boards, internal referrals, your applicant tracking system (ATS), your personal network, your management teams' network, strategic marketing campaigns, social branding and reputation building, catchy job descriptions, staffing firms, and others. Rather than attempt to implement all these verticals immediately, start with a set of three to five that you believe will be the most impactful to your business; choose options you can implement consistently and with results you can measure.

Sit down with your management team and decide what success looks like in each of those chosen verticals. Then create a set of blueprints for each one, drawing up a step-by-step process that your teams will follow to achieve goals. To be certain the verticals you have created are effective, it's extremely important to track them closely. Track every detail of these programs for a significant period, and determine if those methods are worth continuing.

A word of warning here: Make sure that you have given each vertical enough time, that you are running the programs correctly, and that you have consistently followed your blueprint. Oftentimes programs are ended before they have had enough time to take root, or they fail because they were not set up properly or weren't rolled out to the company in a clear and concise manner.

Additionally, some verticals will take longer than others to produce results—so take your time and manage them properly. Have you ever heard of the book *Three Feet from Gold* by Sharon L. Lechter and Greg S. Reid?[3] It states that people tend to give up right before they reach gold—so make sure you give your referral program enough time to take root.

Once you have framed out the process and have followed it successfully for at least two quarters, consider feathering in some other programs. Everything you do needs to be clearly written out, executed properly, and consistently documented and followed.

You must be sure your crew understands the plan and will execute it well. Consistency is critical when building and managing your business.

⌂ PUNCH LIST

- **Develop a plan.** Create a blueprint for recruiting talent and follow it consistently.

- **Find common denominators.** Look at your best hires, and make a list of what they share in common. If they share common background industries or companies, target those areas as fertile recruiting opportunities.

- **Make use of the "brag behind the brand" mentality.** Think: "What do you do?/Where do you work?"

- **Reward your people.** One reliable and cost-saving method for recruiting: Ask your employees to do it for you. As an incentive, reward them for successful referrals.

- **Begin with three to five verticals.** Start out focusing on three to five areas of recruiting. Be consistent. Measure results.

- **Don't give up three feet from gold.** Give your recruitment methods enough time. Gold might be just within reach!

Discover Your Guiding Lights

"One of the greatest values of mentors is the ability
to see ahead what others cannot see and to help them
navigate a course to their destination."

—JOHN C. MAXWELL

A foreman's job is usually the top position within the construction hierarchy, reporting directly to the owner. They are responsible for ensuring that everything goes smoothly on the construction site. In order for you to work *on* the business rather than continually *in* the business, you'll need at least one good foreman—maybe more—depending on the size and nature of your company.

Running your business is all-consuming, and the busier it becomes, the more you will find yourself trapped in the weeds.

You'll spend a great amount of time "in the business" when, in fact, you should be spending most of your time "on the business." In the early years, you'll likely not have a management team to provide guidance and help you grow—it will be you and you only. For an entrepreneur, this is a lonely and frustrating time, as you will struggle for answers to many tough decisions.

Did you ever notice that when someone brings you a problem of their own, it's relatively easy to find a solution, yet solving your own problems often seems insurmountable? That is because we are often trapped in the weeds—the small details—of our own problems and unable to see things clearly, objectively, and without emotion. It's difficult to step away from the business, especially in the early years, which makes it difficult to find the clarity to make the right decisions. Additionally, entrepreneurs sometimes suffer from emotional paralysis, not making right decisions because they are so emotionally attached to someone or something that they can't think rationally.

Growing up, I spent a good amount of time reading. I used to hide under the covers at night with a flashlight long after I was supposed to be asleep. I have always had a thirst to learn and really wanted to create a happy, stable life for myself. I also had a lot of free time on my hands, as my mother worked three jobs. My father spent all of his free time with friends—golfing, drinking, and gambling—so I was pretty much left to fend for myself. When I grew tired of being at my house, I would call up my uncle, and he would come get me.

My aunt and uncle's house was my sanctuary, filled with constant support, enthusiasm, and genuine love. I learned all my life skills there: how to sew, cook, make things, and be a good human being. They were very simple people. My aunt worked as a retail store manager, and my uncle was a painter. They loved me dearly and taught me to respect all people, to always be courteous, and to be kind to everyone. I was my aunt's mentee, and she was bound and determined to teach me every lesson in her possession. My maternal figures taught me there's pride in work, whatever the job may be. Whether it's a large project or a menial task, do it to the very best of your ability. It's got your name on it!

But what really shaped me into the person I am today was the letters. Every morning without fail, on the little wooden desk in my bedroom, I would find a hand-penned letter from my aunt written in ink on the cardboard insert of a pantyhose package. She had beautiful script penmanship and loved blue flair pens. She saved every piece of cardboard that came out of her pantyhose packaging. I laugh now just thinking of her putting those pantyhose on every morning and carefully surrendering the plastic but keeping the white cardboard inserts.

Some days the letters were simple: "You are a wonderful girl who can do anything you set your mind to. I love you $1 million. Love, M." When I was facing a more complex or challenging issue, there were two or three pages. My aunt and I had magnificent communication through her letters of encouragement and strength. I grew accustomed to getting a letter every day, and she never let me down.

Through my school days and after I dropped out and started to work full-time, I still received a daily letter from my aunt. She knew that consistency was extremely important for me. Since I had little consistency with my mother and father, she innately knew that I needed it from her. Those letters showed me the importance of communication and, most importantly, accountability. I was always held accountable for my actions. The punishment for me was feeling her disappointment.

The few times I disappointed my aunt, she would start the conversation with "I am disappointed in you." Those five words would gut me. I never wanted to let anyone down, and I have carried that important responsibility throughout my life. There is power in words. When someone makes you think about and be accountable for your actions, that's when true learning begins.

As a leader, you are given a choice on how you want to address and engage your employees. There are those leaders who choose to yell, intimidate, and instill fear, and those who choose to nurture, discuss, mentor, and grow their people. My upbringing included perfect examples of both. It's much harder and more time-consuming to be patient and constructive than it is to simply yell at someone—or passively aggressively ignore them—and walk away. However, the long-term results of that hard work will yield a greater return on your employee investment.

Say No to Yes-Men and Yes-Women

Being a leader is often lonely and isolating. When you need answers, you often have nowhere to turn or no one appropriate to ask. The last thing you want to do is start discussing dire and critical issues with your employees. Trying to resolve these larger issues on your own is frustrating and emotionally draining.

You will want to align yourself with experts in areas where you lack knowledge or expertise to maximize your firm's success.

As you start out, it is critically important to realize that you will not be good at everything. It is okay to ask for help. Becoming comfortable asking for assistance will make the difference in getting from good to great.

Additionally, each time you hire, look to hire someone smarter than you. You can't let your ego stand in the way of hiring people who are more intelligent, more skilled, or more educated than you are; this would be an epic mistake. You'll want a staff that is confident in suggesting new ideas and providing strategic ways to grow your business. You'll need and want their input. Hiring a bunch of people who are "yes-men/women" or mediocre will hurt—or at least stall—the progress of your business.

Hiring yes-men/women will limit your ability to be challenged and to see things differently. Allowing your manager- and executive-level colleagues to only agree with you is unacceptable. Your firm will lack innovation, and you will not have anyone in the company who can take up the slack when you fall short. And believe me, everyone falls short at one point or another. There's no shame in recognizing this.

Every leader has strengths and weaknesses. For your firm to be a strong and balanced organization, you'll need people whose strengths complement your weaknesses. Additionally, yes-men/women aren't honest; they don't give you the authentic feedback and candor you desperately need to build and run something successful. It could cost you big.

You want people who can challenge you, will push you creatively, and won't quietly fall in line and join the consensus. If your leaders are yes-men/women and you come up with an idea that is bad, they will likely agree, and you will all go down the rabbit hole together and take the company with you. Instead, fill your company with women and men who are innovators, who exercise good judgment, and aren't afraid to ask questions. Fill your firm with exceptional talent. And don't settle for less-than-optimal hires.

How do you find this talent? We discussed some options in the previous chapter, but here I want to focus on taking your time to get things right. This starts with creating sustainable processes that allow you to hire the right people over and over. As I said, take the time to get this right.

1. **Hire right first.** Do not panic and hire someone simply to fill a seat. Make sure you put the right person in the right seat. Your business will suffer more with the wrong person in the wrong seat, and the decision will be costly.

2. **Mistakes are expensive.** The cost of a bad hire can reach up to 30 percent of the employee's first-year earnings. Broken down, these costs relate to hiring, pay, and retention. Seventy-four percent of companies who made a poor hire lost an average of $14,900 per poor hire.[1]

3. **A bad hire results in a decline in morale.** Every time you bring the wrong person into your business, you affect morale at your company and create doubt among your staff. It's like the way an earthquake affects the foundation of your house; it starts with small hairline cracks, and eventually the foundation starts to break down and crumble. A bad hire unsettles everything and messes up the flow and vibe of your company.

Your people are critically important to the success and growth of your firm. You need to seek support from your employees while you direct, recruit, and network to find the right person. Ask your staff to pitch in until you find the best hire for the position.

Oftentimes, all I had to do was ask my staff to help, and they were more than happy to do so; many employees are eager to add new skills to their résumé. Alternatively, there are many creative ways to fill a gap—consultants and part-time workers—while you take the time and hire properly.

Reinforce Your Shortcomings

When the time comes to hire an executive for your firm, look at your shortcomings. It's best to showcase your strengths and hire for the areas where there are the greatest weaknesses. And remember: Admitting your weaknesses isn't itself a weakness but a strength, as it helps you fill possible gaps in your company's overall competency.

My area of weakness is numbers. I am most comfortable with communicating a vision, innovating, connecting, engaging, and selling our products and services to the world. To complement my area of weakness, a strong CFO or controller was the best addition to our firm. If you can't afford these types of positions in your company, consider bringing in consultants to help you bridge the gap. In addition, I strongly recommend that you invest a great deal of time in recruiting and retaining the most talented sales and business development people to drive the sales revenue at your firm.

Remind yourself how long it took you to recruit and retain your employees. They are your *best* people—and not just your top performers but your most valuable and culturally aligned people. You will find that many of your top executives will become mentors to you as well. You will be surprised by what they can do for you when you need them—often when you least expect it.

I remember one year we were in a dire situation at our company, but I had promised one of my most valuable leaders a $20,000 bonus. It was a time when issuing this bonus would have been very difficult to do. But my employees were very dear to me—especially this one—so I managed to move many things around and issue this bonus.

Treat your people right, be honest with them, communicate, and build a culture that will retain your top performers.

That Monday, when I came into work, I found an envelope under my door with the check and a note from this employee saying, "I really appreciate this bonus, but I know the company is going through tough times right now. Please return this to the company and catch me next year. I'm here to help and provide my support wherever and whenever you need it."

Consult Your Committee

Once your firm is established and stable, it would be wise to join an advisory group. There are many options available to you: Renaissance Executive Forum, Vistage, YEO—Young Entrepreneurs Organization—most with local chapters and international connections. A recent study of executive coaching in a Fortune 500 firm by MetrixGlobal reported a 529 percent return on investment and significant tangible benefits to the business. A survey by Manchester Inc. of one hundred executives found that coaching provided an average return on investment of almost six times the cost of coaching.[2]

What might surprise you the most is that the challenges you struggle with are almost identical to what other entrepreneurs struggle with. You might think you're alone, but you're not. Having an advisory group or a monthly mentoring group of trusted advisors is one of the best investments you can make—in yourself and in your business. These folks will help you swiftly navigate the emotional decisions you need to make to move your business forward, and they will give you the ideas and straightforward advice you need.

There are many examples I can share about the value I gained from being a member of my advisory group, but one example stands out. I had a director who had been with my firm for more than fifteen years. He started out exemplary but declined over the years because of many personal challenges that negatively impacted his performance. At the end of the day, he just wasn't performing up to the expectations of our company, and his negativity started to overshadow his performance. Additionally, he had become a detractor, infecting our culture. We offered him counseling, I personally worked with him one-on-one, we offered him coaching services, but nothing changed.

Because he had been with me from almost the beginning, I was having a terrible time making the right decision to terminate his employment. And I knew he was staying with the company solely because he was extremely loyal to me. This was a time when I needed to do the brave work and move these employees into happy. Decisions like these seem so obvious and easy afterward, yet they often leave us paralyzed by emotional distress as we work our way through them.

In one of our monthly advisory meetings, I brought my concerns about this employee to the attention of my peers. They broke down the issue with me in thirty minutes by asking "defining questions" to get the answers they needed to reach an informed—and, if possible, unanimous—decision. The undisputed advice was to terminate this employee immediately. There was no emotion; they told me directly and very matter-of-factly what needed to be done.

I can assure you, I had no yes-men/women in that monthly advisor group. I was thankful for their honesty. This is what you need to gain clarity in order to make proper decisions for your company. Additionally, my peers held me accountable by ensuring I planned the process and exact date of termination so I remained committed to the plan.

When I returned to the office after the meeting that day, I immediately went to my vice president of human resources and started the process of termination. I followed through on my commitment and terminated this employee on the very day I promised I would. It was emotional and upsetting, but it was also one of the best decisions I made for the company—and for the employee. He and I are still very good friends; he has completely turned his life around and is extremely happy doing something he thoroughly loves.

Interpreting challenging issues for others is quite easy because there is no emotional investment for you. Yet navigating your own business and making these emotional decisions for yourself can be crippling, and it's tempting to ignore them, with the hope they go away or resolve themselves on their own. But that's not the way to move your company forward.

Finding like-minded entrepreneurs and selecting the right people to support and represent you will make a huge difference to the outcomes at your firm.

What's especially helpful about a network of like-minded peers is that they likely have already experienced many of the challenges and issues you might be faced with, especially if their firms are significantly larger than yours. This can include staffing but also other aspects of your company, such as new software, technology, or best practices in other areas. Perhaps they've upgraded their entire accounting software platform, or they've implemented a new process like the Entrepreneurial Operating System and can guide you through all the data, choices, and information they already reviewed, saving you a tremendous number of wasted hours, painstaking decisions, and potential wrong outcomes.

Whatever stage you find yourself in—start-up, small business, or midsize to large—there are always like-minded people you can network with. If you don't have the financial resources, consider calling some of your friends, tapping into your network, asking your customers, or starting with a local chamber of commerce. There is always a directory available that you can use to make some of these calls.

The best part—valuable business partners, colleagues, and coaches will tell you the truth, even if you hate hearing it!

⌂ PUNCH LIST

- **Hire right first.** If you hire right, you avoid a lot of problems. Take the time to get it right.

- **Reinforce Your Shortcomings.** Complement your weaknesses by hiring to help bolster areas where you may fall short.

- **Say no to yes-men/women.** Don't surround yourself with yes-men and women, or you'll miss out on the very talents you hired your people to provide! You'll stagnate or even falter.

- **Find your guiding light.** There are many groups out there willing to mentor newbies. Or hire an executive coach. Studies show the expense is worth it.

- **Consult your committee.** Give them honest information, and trust them to put the company's best interests first when they make their recommendations.

Find Power in Persistence

"I've learned that people will forget what you said,
people will forget what you did, but people will
never forget how you made them feel."

—MAYA ANGELOU

How do you differentiate a good builder from a great one? The devil is in the details. Anyone who knows anything about construction can walk through a renovation and see shortcuts and missteps compared to superior quality work. There is a difference between a clean site and an unkempt one. Once wooden floors are sanded, they should be thoroughly covered to ensure they maintain their new integrity as they await their finished coat. Paint should always be done after the floors are sanded; otherwise, you will have a dusty mess on your hands.

A high-end general contractor will have someone on site each day to clean up at day's end after the plumbers, electricians, carpenters, and painters leave, allowing the expert tradesmen to focus on what they do best and work more efficiently. Remodeling is a well-orchestrated dance and should follow an extremely defined process, much like the sales process.

Let's face it: Anything you could ever want or need today is available with a few clicks of your mouse. Or better yet, just ask Alexa; Google will find it no matter what or where it is. Something you order today will be at your doorstep tomorrow. Great ideas and services are popping up overnight everywhere, so having a strong plan to serve and engage your customers is paramount. Remember: Being good is merely the entry fee for business today. You must be exceptional!

When I set out to open my staffing firm thirty-two years ago, I was twenty-two years old. Having left school early and working full-time at such a young age, I felt as if I already had a lifetime of experience under my belt! Growing up so independently, seeing what I had seen, and having to find the resources I needed for myself, I felt confident I could do the research and invest the focus and determination necessary to successfully build my own firm. These qualities helped me a great deal when I launched my own company because I was accustomed to working with very little. I spent a great deal of time self-educating, and since I had developed such a strong passion for reading, I was able to find most of what I needed to aid me in the creation of my business.

When I started my staffing firm, there were plenty of strong competitors in the market. By then, I had been working for one of the best firms for three years myself. I was determined to examine each business, find out as much as I could about every aspect of their services, and then find new and better ways to run and operate my own firm. Many fledgling entrepreneurs simply open a competing firm and lower their prices. I would have no part of that model, as "in the absence of value, customers will defer to price." The last thing you want to become is a commoditized business model continually lowering your price to win business.

Follow the Money

As I talk to other business owners and witness how many businesses serve their customers today, I see many gaps in their processes, beginning with lack of follow-up, which allows potential revenue to just slip away. A good friend of mine told me of a continual issue his firm was faced with. He owns a large plumbing supply company with multiple locations that actively receive daily orders by phone and in person. Since they distribute all types of plumbing, heating, and air-conditioning products, they have thousands of parts in a huge 200,000-square-foot warehouse.

Each day their inbound customer care department and sales personnel receive calls and emails asking for quotes for potential jobs. These jobs could consist of a single boiler, a full bathroom remodel, or the outfitting of an entire apartment complex of four hundred units. Quoting orders like these is time-consuming and takes knowledgeable, trained people. If I had to guess, some of these large quotes take hours to complete, as the parts and build-out can be quite intricate. When the president dug into their sales process, he discovered that the quotes were, in fact, provided to the customers, but they weren't followed up on with consistency. This meant his firm was missing out on valuable sales.

This lack of follow-up can cost a firm 25 percent or more in potential lost revenue. Because my plumbing-supplier friend is a highly process-oriented and observant entrepreneur, he remedied the problem by creating a detailed, systematic follow-up process and increased sales by 20 percent. Follow-up is so important; one study shows that a full 80 percent of potential sales opportunities are lost simply due to lack of follow-up.[1]

When considering the growth of your business, develop a strong conversion process to turn customer inquiries into customer quotes and unfilled orders into filled ones. Each time a customer called our staffing firm to inquire about a potential candidate or job order, we created a record. We managed these records diligently, and we ensured prompt and consistent human follow-up.

Notice that I said "human" follow-up. Today, there are so many ways to manage a customer inquiry, especially through technology. The issue with all this great technology is that no one diligently follows up by phone anymore.

BEWARE THE SALES VS. MARKETING WARS

When my company was purchased, the acquiring firm had a marketing department of four people. They were a talented team dedicated to providing us with data about new customer leads, placement ratios, and other divisions' customers. They had a lot of useful data that could have been used to cultivate additional revenue.

At that time, I was asked to be the chief marketing officer in addition to my role as president. I was elated at the chance to work with this team, as I had always known the value of a partnership between sales and marketing. This team of four was extremely bright, eager, well researched, and ready to increase business. They were model employees and 100 percent culturally aligned with the MVPs of the company. They had so much valuable data, but you know what? No one bothered to follow up on any of it. No one saw the value.

It was mind-blowing and quite frustrating. Day after day, this team diligently showed me a variety of ways to capture this valuable data, and no one paid any attention to it or used any of it. Salespeople were handed warm leads daily, but no one bothered to follow up on those leads and make calls. It drove me nuts, and it drove the team nuts! They could not understand it, I could not understand it, and those four team members became disenchanted.

People do their best work when they understand their job and what's going on in the company. They need to have at least a general sense of the "why" and the "what" of their work. If marketing had taken the time to actually show sales where the data was coming from, how they gathered the results, and where sales could influence and use these results, I believe that data would have been viewed as much more beneficial. The work of that team would have been appreciated and valued.

PROVIDE THE "WHY" AND THE "WHAT"

Salespeople do not want to look foolish to their customers or work off of blind results. Because our sales team didn't know the "what" or "why," they chose to ignore the materials altogether. I also think there is an assumption bias about different departments. In some cases, marketing is assumed to be more creative and based on aesthetics, whereas sales is based more on instinct and personality. What I really know to be true is that both divisions are fact-based. Of course, your personality might get you in the door for a sales call, but the final sale is supported by facts and data.

If marketing and sales had created open communication between the two departments, a significant number of leads would have turned into sales. Marketing had the data and reports to prove there were areas of potential customer acquisitions, and sales had the skill set and teams to turn these customer acquisitions into actual sales.

A systematic process should have been followed. But the sales managers always claimed to be too busy to add these simple follow-up calls into their pipeline, even though the calls could potentially result in new prospective customers and lots of additional revenue for the company! Had they taken the time to feather these leads into their existing daily calls, I guarantee they would have increased sales and garnered many new customers.

Take every valuable bit of data, create a process, and follow it up diligently, efficiently, and consistently!

Each division manager could have easily taken this data and created a systematic process to delegate these leads, grade or score them, input them into the customer relationship management system (CRM), and diligently follow up. Oftentimes, I have found that salespeople take the simplest of situations and create the greatest resistance. These were extremely "warm" leads; they were customers who had experience with us and knew us well. Why we would let all this great data go to waste—and allow the customer to miss out—was beyond my understanding.

YOU'RE NEVER TOO BUSY TO FOLLOW UP ON A LEAD

These were all key performance indicators (KPIs) that marketing was generating weekly, along with so many other pieces of valuable data that could have increased our sales exponentially, yet no one saw the value in using them. Obvious leads and potential new sales opportunities were given to heads of departments but were never followed up on. Marketing always took the time to follow up with sales, but generally, sales either never responded back or claimed they were too busy. Tell me: When is someone ever too busy to follow up on potential business? The salespeople I know wouldn't let an obvious opportunity go unattended.

My crack marketing team grew more discouraged because their brilliant ideas and presentations were rarely utilized. This opened my eyes to why there is often a combative climate between sales and marketing departments. A true home run for companies would be to marry their sales and marketing departments and show each of them the value they provide to one another. This would increase sales significantly. I often ask myself why people couldn't see the importance of focusing on sales, follow-up, and customer satisfaction. After all, we were running a *sales* business!

I don't mean to beat a dead horse, but I can't tell you how many times a day I witnessed extremely obvious opportunities for follow-up simply evaporate, without anyone paying attention to the massive loss of sales that no doubt followed.

Here are some convincing statistics on the importance of follow-up and the tenacity and perseverance of salespeople:

SALES STATISTICS

48% of salespeople never follow up with a prospect.

25% of salespeople make a second contact and stop.

12% of salespeople only make three contacts and stop.

10% of salespeople make more than three contacts.

2% of sales are made on the first contact.

3% of sales are made on the second contact.

5% of sales are made on the third contact.

10% of sales are made on the fourth contact.

80% of sales are made on the fifth to twelfth contact.

Eighty-eight percent of salespeople give up after four "no's," leaving only 12 percent who follow up the fifth time! One can infer that 12 percent of salespeople are getting 80 percent of the sales simply by consistently following up.[3]

If you feel bold enough to speak with your customers, ask them about their buying choices; ask them who they buy from and why. They will quite often tell you that they simply didn't hear back from anyone, so they called a competitor. Salespeople think it is something grander that motivates buyers, but the statistics show that lost sales are mostly due to lack of follow-up. The one who answers the call gets the business.

We must commit to speaking with our customers regularly about their businesses and their needs. Quite often, salespeople spend time cultivating new sales prospects when business is already right under their noses with their existing customers. *Salespeople make their job harder than it needs to be!*

The probability of selling to an existing customer is 60 to 70 percent. The probability of selling to a new prospect is 5 to 20 percent. Sixty-five percent of a company's business comes from existing customers.[4]

Additionally, when a customer asks for a quote or places an order, a strategic process should be followed to ensure diligent follow-up. This might sound rudimentary, but I promise you, I increased our sales revenue by 10 to 15 percent just by following up on each one of these calls.

Cultivating strong relationships and delivering an exceptional product should be your top priority 24/7. You should always be thinking obsessively about your customers: "How can I help my customer? What are my customer's pain points? How can I help my customer overcome this challenge? Do they need talent in this area?" Every thought and strategy should be about your customers.

Devise a system that works for your business. What worked best for our firm was to categorize our customers and prospects by size. This gave us the ability to judge how often we could acceptably contact them. Then we created a variety of scripts and tools to help our salespeople perform their jobs. We also researched and found specific hard-to-hire talent and provided this information to our customers.

> *A balance is needed between cultivating and building new business, and protecting and growing existing business.*

By evaluating your target customers, you can clearly see which customers are utilizing your services to the fullest and which are not. This allows you to expand your services and products and build stronger, more profitable customer relationships.

SALES ACQUISITION WORKSHEET

Ways to grow company revenue and build sales relationships
1. List all existing customers and routinely and systematically call to sell them your services:
2. List all existing customers and routinely and systematically call to sell them "new" products or services that they might not have knowledge of:

continued

3. List all prospective customers and routinely and
   systematically call to sell additional products/services:

   _____   _____

   _____   _____

   _____   _____

4. Offer additional products/services to prospective customers:

   _____   _____

   _____   _____

   _____   _____

5. Research customers that you haven't called in six months
   and re-introduce your products/services to them:

   _____   _____

   _____   _____

   _____   _____

6. Call "lost customers" that used to buy from you
   and re-introduce your products/services to them:

   _____   _____

   _____   _____

   _____   _____

7. Call your "best" customers and ask them for two referrals that
   they know who might be able to use your products/services:

   _____   _____

   _____   _____

   _____   _____

In sales, you are either solving a problem, fulfilling a want, providing the customer with a better product, or making the customer's job easier. Customers don't buy products—they buy solutions to their problems. Take the time to create a process for these scenarios, and you will have happy and enthusiastic customers.

Go Live!

People are busier than ever these days. Human resources departments are often shorthanded, with staff members doing the jobs of two or three people. They need trusted, reliable advisors to help them cut through all the candidate traffic and administrative efforts that fall under the recruitment process. They will always find time for you if you offer them value and prove to them that you are a trusted advisor.

To get customers to value your services, you must prove to them that you are worthy of their business. So many recruiting firms call potential customers and ask if they have any openings to fill. This is just embarrassing to the staffing industry. They do not know you, and you do not know what they need. You have not established a relationship, earned their trust, or proven that you are competent or of value to them, and you do not have any information about their MVPs. Why would this firm work with you? You lose credibility if you work in this manner.

So how do you garner trust and build sustainable relationships with your customers? By using the phone, creating a human connection, and following up as you promised. Ninety-two percent of all customer interactions happen over the phone.[5] Many salespeople use email as their main point of contact and are discouraged from or afraid to pick up the phone and speak to a live person. I wonder how much business is being lost because of this. And since it takes an average of eight cold call attempts to reach a prospect, I also imagine a lot of salespeople today are not bringing in new customers.

Why are salespeople so afraid to communicate with their customers? Because they don't believe that customers want to hear from them or because they don't think they have anything of value to offer. Salespeople need to research and rehearse the calls they make to customers. No one should just pick up the phone and wing it without researching ideas and solutions for their customers. Practicing makes people better, and salespeople should do this to improve. Once you perfect your calls, you must be persistent, consistent, and use multiple tools and ways to reach your customers. However, nothing should ever prevent you from calling your customers to see how they are, to check in and let them know you care about your relationship.

It is my experience that young people are particularly hesitant to use the phone to speak with customers. Younger people tend to story-tell through social media, where they control not only the content but the visual experience. When you post something socially, you have the opportunity to tweak and perfect every word, whereas when you are on a call, this must come fluidly and naturally through rehearsal. The balance of both worlds might be video calls. This is an opportunity to take advantage of the younger generation, allowing them to utilize the technologies they are most comfortable with to reach like-minded peers.

There are many ways to create engagement with customers. Keep an open mind about the wide variety of options.

Know Thy Customer

If you are fortunate enough to land a face-to-face meeting with a potential customer, respect that their time is of great value. You must offer them value in return—and quickly—before they lose interest in your presentation altogether. Oftentimes, a salesperson may manage to get in front of customers who are desperate to find a competent partner, but then this valuable customer-facing time is wasted on meaningless blather.

I hate to say this, but we had a salesperson who did just this. She talked nonstop about our company, rambling on about all our services and divisions to a potential customer, going over every vertical we had (even if the customer didn't hire for that vertical), and then—if time permitted—she asked the customer about *their* needs! To be valuable to your customers, you must become intimately acquainted with their issues and understand their frustrations and pain points.

Salespeople may think they need to talk. But they'll be more successful by listening.

Listen to learn.
Don't listen to answer.

A great salesperson must *suffer through the silence*! Caring and competent salespeople do much more listening, probing, and question asking than talking. Start by asking a lot of questions that cannot obviously be found through research, and then suffer through the silence by remaining quiet while your customers tell you what you really need to hear!

Research is easier than ever these days. You can learn about a customer's hiring history, their retention, the struggles and challenges they are currently facing, what their culture is like, and the "why" of their firm. Why would an employee want to work there? Why XYZ company over ABC company? What is their sizzle? Research their competitors and what they are doing. How do they compare? Additionally, you need to know if the MVPs really exist and if they're followed and promoted consistently throughout the entire organization.

Since my firm was connecting with talent daily, we were always able to find out rather swiftly which customers were exceptional and which were mediocre. You can go to Glassdoor and read reviews. Gather insights on your customers' social impression, and bring this information to the meeting. You can also research your own firm's reputation. You might be having a hard time attracting talent and not be aware that your social reputation needs improvement.

Be a Purple Squirrel

Additionally, your company must prove to your customers that you are different. Outline why you are the purple squirrel—unusual, unique, rare—a stand-out from your competitors. At my firm, we had a recruiting strategy and talent optimization process that helped firms improve their talent and returned time and cost savings back to our customers.

Demonstrating your value to customers takes a long time and should be done with consistent and measured efforts. It is vital to put yourself in your customer's position. Understand that they are getting pressured every day to provide lower costs, faster delivery, diversified products, and so on. Therefore, it is paramount to maintain consistent contact with your customers. You must showcase your successes and progress quarterly to your customers and thereby prove your worth.

Bring a presentation with your quarterly successes, and show your customer the amount of money you saved them, the time you returned to them, and the effort and pain you removed from them. Customers need to be reminded of these accomplishments; they quickly forget and are extremely busy. Routinely remind them of the high-quality work you are doing for them, show them you are a strategic partner, and present evidence so that they can defend your partnership with the firm if someone questions your relationship.

Make yourself so valuable they could not possibly consider losing your support.

⌂ PUNCH LIST

- **Prioritize quality over quantity.** Become known for your quality; don't fall into a race to become the cheapest provider.

- **Humanize the experience.** Respond to customers with actual human phone calls. The one who answers the call gets the business.

- **Adapt to technology.** If younger employees prefer connecting with customers through video calls or other tech, keep an open mind.

- **Beware the sales vs. marketing wars.** Marry the two departments, create alignment, and improve sales acquisitions.

- **Remember that customers don't buy products; they buy solutions.** Make sure you ask what the customer needs, research a good solution, and then follow up by providing it.

- **Listen to learn.** Be present and listen when your customers talk. Don't listen to respond; listen to understand.

- **Use your "Sales Acquisition Worksheet."** Prove your worth to existing and prospective customers. Make your company's services and products indispensable.

- **Be the purple squirrel.** Find unique and rare attributes and value propositions that your company can offer to differentiate you from competitors.

Commit to Consistency

"Many of life's failures are people who did not realize
how close they were to success when they gave up."

—THOMAS EDISON

Painting is a relatively easy process. It is simple to figure out and can change an entire room with an afternoon's effort. However, did you ever watch a painter paint? Sixty percent of a painter's job is preparing, while only 40 percent of the work is the physical act of painting. To have a meticulous paint job become a reality, you need someone who has done a lot of prep work and pays extraordinary attention to detail. Furniture must be moved and covered, door handles and switch plates must be removed, windows and trim must all be taped off, and floors must be protected. Taping off the trim of a room can take a long time and must be done perfectly, or you will get bleed through, and the line that meets your wall and trim will look as if it was done by an amateur.

Think of your salespeople as your painters, expending most of their time—60 percent of it—preparing and only 40 percent on actual face-to-face sales. There won't be any sales without focused and consistent preparation.

Anyone who's worked for or with me knows I have an unrelenting passion for serving the customer. Early in my business career, I developed a disciplined process for sales, customer engagement, and follow-up calls. I was the salesperson who never missed an assigned customer check-in, always touched base the day I said I would, and sustained the sales cycle through to the bitter end, while most others fell off early or midway through the engagement process. By making every call diligently and systematically, exactly when I was scheduled to do so, I demonstrated that customers could count on me. I earned their trust, and they depended and relied on me.

The Magic Bullet

Most salespeople do not understand that customers are secretly testing us. Customers do not rush to return our initial call because they know we most likely will not call again. Most salespeople give up after their very first call, and customers know this. On average, salespeople need to make five or six phone calls to have a successful cold call conversion. Also, it takes an average of eight attempts before agents reach a lead who is willing to talk.[1]

The fact that most salespeople don't bother calling more than once is mind-blowing! Salespeople might not do this intentionally— they get distracted or busy—but they do it regardless of the reason, and their results suffer. Customers expect to be called multiple times and deserve this level of service. Salespeople need to be consistent in order to garner trust so that customers can see the value of their services and products.

In addition, customers listen to the delivery and content of our sales calls and wait to see if we will call again . . . and again.

Competition steals away your business every time—simply because you did not make the call!

I've been on both sides of the sales-customer relationship. I used to receive plenty of sales calls to our firm. I would listen to the content and structure of the call, determine whether the salesperson offered value, then hold out for consistent follow-up calls. I would return the calls of the rare few who would consistently call me (three to five times). I respect and value people who abide by a systematic process and stick with their intentions. I also have a deep admiration for diligent and persistent salespeople. They know their audience and understand that customers are getting calls all day long. People are bombarded with emails, newsletters, and an overwhelming amount of social content daily. My sales staff frequently asked me, "How can I get XYZ customer on the phone? How can I get their attention? What can I say that will get them to call me back or do business with me?"

I used to tease my colleagues and tell them I needed to consult with my Magic 8-Ball to give them the answer. Everybody wants the magic bullet—the quick fix. Turn on any channel, and there is a pill that will make you lose fifty pounds or increase your brain octane by 50 percent! We all want quick results without putting in the hard labor. Why is it when someone loses a significant amount of weight, the first question we always ask is, "How did you do it?" Has anyone ever answered, "By eating chocolate cake"? Of course not. It is achieved through consistent and diligent hard work, motivation, diet, and exercise. *Change nothing, and nothing changes.*

The best solutions come through focused, consistent behavior. Think about it for a minute: Don't you think your customers want someone who will call when they say they will and deliver what they say they will when they promise it? Don't you think customers want an easy process, the ability to work with someone they like, and to receive outstanding products and services? Of course they do—especially your established customers. It's what they deserve! They want to work with you—they need you. They want you to call them and tell them about your latest and greatest products. They want a partner that will regularly make them look good and add value to their company. They want someone who will help them eliminate their pain points, resolve their problems, and fix their issues. But for some reason, salespeople often don't do these things. If you are not consistent, do not do routine follow-up, and do not investigate placed orders or quotes given, you will let customers walk away!

To bypass this frustration and loss of revenue in your firm, you must set up a consistent sales process from day one and mandate that your entire firm follow it. Start by creating customer-engagement triggers for your salespeople for consistent follow-up. Here are some ideas.

Customers want to work with someone who will do what they say they are going to do. You must keep your promises.

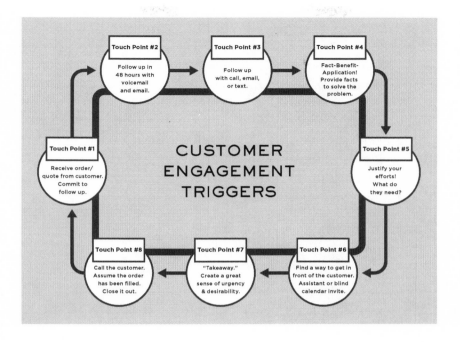

- **Touch Point One**—Receive order/quote from customer. Dialogue with customer. End call with committed action plan, and commit to follow up in no more than forty-eight hours.

- **Touch Point Two**—Call customer. Reiterate commitment from Trigger One. Send follow-up email to customer.

- **Touch Point Three**—Call again. Add valuable content. Reference prior message and commitment at outset of engagement. Send follow-up email to customer.

- **Touch Point Four**—Discuss facts, benefits, and application. Consider which facts can solve their pain points, reiterate the benefits of working together, and review your implementation plan. Send follow-up email to customer.

- **Touch Point Five**—Confirm they still have the need. Offer varied options and try different tactics (e.g., call early in the morning or later in the evening, or ask for a quick face-to-face meeting). Follow up with email to customer.

- **Touch Point Six**—Be creatively careful. Call additional people in the firm. If you can, text them. Try to find out why they aren't returning the call and how you can expedite the process. Remind them: "I want to help you. How can I help?" Create a sense of urgency. Follow up with email to customer.

- **Touch Point Seven**—Try the takeaway method (someone else wants what they asked for). Inform them that they are about to lose their solution, and apply your greatest sense of urgency here. Follow up with an email to customer.

- **Touch Point Eight**—Call the customer and advise them that you are closing out the order if you don't hear from them by 5 p.m. today.

This is merely a sample of touch points that you can put right into your CRM system or create a manual system. You can set up flags in your database or even your calendar to help organize your follow-ups.

But for consistency, you must make a "no exceptions" rule, or slowly, over time, your process will erode and break down. (I'll talk more about this in Lesson 10: Experience Chaos to Find Clarity.) It is critical to have a process—a simple, organized tasking system—for systematic follow-up on every order, quote, or inquiry. There must also be a consistent process for orders accepted to check on the arrival of goods and the services of those goods. I was brutal and relentless about this.

Growing up the way I did, I liked having control over whatever I could. I controlled and owned each of my jobs and always turned in my projects ahead of time. This afforded me time to improve on something if I did not get it quite right. I taught my daughter the same thing, and I believe she would tell you it is one of the best lessons I have given her. By turning in her college papers or projects early and having an intentional conversation with her professor, she had time to implement new ideas and redo something if it was not quite perfect.

I carried this standard to my office. On the first day that each of our consultants started out in the field at a customer's, I mandated a follow-up call be made to both the deployed consultant and to our customer. I used to get a lot of pushback from my staff on this.

I would hear the following excuses: "No news is good news," or "The customer will call us if there is a problem," or "It's too early for feedback." These are examples of salespeople who do not understand the sales process and do not see the value and power of consistency and good follow-up practices. This mentality is nearsighted because it does not consider potential problems that could arise in the future.

Instead, think about the customer's point of view. When you follow up early, you are establishing a process: fulfilling a promise and commitment to excellence. By showing your customers that you care, you are instilling trust, and you are potentially intercepting problems in the very beginning stages. You are negating the possibility of your customer saying later, "You never called and checked in with us." Eighty percent of your future profits will come from just 20 percent of your existing customers.[2]

Think about it. How many times have you purchased something yet never again heard from that salesperson? Salespeople are known for making a sale and then running away or moving on to the next customer. The way to retain loyal customers is to be there for them every step of the way to mitigate any potential issues that might arise. You must understand the value of being a caring provider, of lending an ear if there is a problem that needs to be addressed. And every time you speak to a customer, you must recognize that you have an opportunity to engage with your customer. Every single time I placed our talent into a new job opportunity, I saw the possibilities of future business, of solving a future problem for my customers by providing an early solution. I ended each call with this one simple question: "I would be remiss if I didn't ask you, are there any additional job opportunities that I could currently help you with?"

That's it. That's the magic. Big letdown, right? You're thinking, *Really? That's it? Seems like there's no magic in that question.* But guess what? It increased our sales by 20 to 30 percent annually year over year and won me remarkable customer retention—because I asked, relentlessly, every single time, and then I waited and *listened.* If I heard, "Well, nothing right now," my response would then be, "Not now? I detect that there might be a challenge or opportunity down the road. Is this something that we can discuss now to potentially mitigate any issues for you later?"

I made the call. I asked— and I listened. That is the power of consistency.

The best advice I can give you is to spend a lot of time creating a process for your sales and engagement services. Remember, you must follow the blueprints for sales and talent processes—beginning with the initial quote, to the order, into the delivery—from beginning to end. And then repeat, because you are never done. There should always be something to ask your customers about, to discuss, to help and assist them with.

Remember to ask open-ended questions like "Did you know

that . . . ?" "What happens when . . . ?" "What is the reasoning behind . . . ?" There is always more for a customer to learn about your firm. Look for areas where you can bring value to your customers by offering any and all services you have available to help them solve a problem, grow their firm, or add talent to their organization. Your service and support efforts to your customers should never wane.

Talk to the Ones That Got Away

When you lose an order to a competitor, you should have the same follow-up process that you would if you had filled it. I cannot tell you how much business that brought to our firm. Customers used to be mystified and confused when we'd call after losing a sale. They would ask, "Why are you calling? You didn't even make the placement?" I would say I was calling because I cared, because I was committed to service and to making sure my customers were happy regardless of who made the sale.

It costs sixteen times more to nurture a new customer up to the same level of revenue contribution as an existing customer.[3] The next time that customer had an order to fill, who do you think they called? You might lose one order; don't lose two! Sales is about creating opportunities and building trusting relationships. Sales is about relentless service. Few salespeople will go to this level of follow-up. As we learned, at least half give up after the first call. Very few will go after business they lost. But they should. I did it all the time, and it created award-winning relationships and a deep respect from my customers. If you think about your process, you will find numerous opportunities to make an impression with your customers—all you must do is ask! Ask, "Are you okay? Is there anything I can provide you with that will make your job, life, or career better, happier, or easier?"

There are two kinds of salespeople. What kind are you going to be?

⌂ PUNCH LIST

- **Stay persistent.** Follow through, keep calling, and stay the course. No excuses.

- **Remember that customers need you.** Customers want to work with you; in fact, they need you.

- **Execute all triggers.** Consider the list of eight customer-engagement "triggers" for consistent follow-up.

- **Always be present.** Retain customers and create a loyal base by being there for the customer every step of the way.

- **Ask questions to find solutions.** There's always something you can ask your customers about or help them with. Ask, and be sure to *listen*.

- **Lose one sale, never two.** When you lose out to a competitor, call the customer anyway. Pursue the same follow-up process that you would if you had filled that order.

- **Be reliable, present, and valuable.** Always ask if you can do more. Even if you lose a sale, you might get that opportunity back, or you might get another sale down the line.

PART 3

Execution

Geneneral contractors tend to have a bad reputation for not being on time or consistent throughout the duration of a construction project. Over the years, I have worked with countless general contractors, architects, remodelers, and tradespeople. I have met the good, the mediocre, and a few of the very worst remodelers.

My husband and I have done thirteen renovations, including new builds and a few corporate buildings. Our most recent remodel was a large renovation and rebuild that was all-consuming. It was an existing structure that I was insistent about preserving, and it needed to be completely gutted and remodeled, including a full addition and a brand-new barn. The general contractor I worked with, Tom Kane, taught me a great deal about pride in work, consistency, and the ability to please customers even in the worst of times. He also taught me that there are excellent tradespeople who do know how to respond to customers in a timely fashion.

Every morning at 7:15 a.m., the first pop of the nail gun would fill our house, and the day began. We could set our watch by the arrival of Tom's crew. Every single day for the duration of their time on our job, that first pop of their nail gun was our morning wake-up call.

Planning the Impression

"You have to treat everyone you meet as if they are the most important person in the world—because they are. If not to you, then to someone; and if not today, then perhaps tomorrow."

—LINDA KAPLAN THALER AND ROBIN KOVAL

I lived by this mantra. When I opened the doors of my firm, I was committed to providing this level of attentiveness to every one of my customers. Service is about meeting the needs of others. But it goes deeper than that. Service, along with creating an impression and experience, is about how you show up and act every day in front of your colleagues, employees, peers, and customers. You control you—your behaviors, your impressions, and whether you are going to follow through and do what you say you will do.

Serving well is about painting a picture, creating a lasting impression, evoking or awakening something in someone that they will cherish—or at least remember for a long time. It goes way beyond making a call or following up with a customer. It's a deeply rooted understanding that you are creating an experience that will stay with your customer long after you fulfill their order.

As a leader, you may see quite clearly the importance of embracing the highest level of customer service, but how do you infuse this into your culture and people? Salespeople are considered the superheroes of an organization. They are the revenue generators and, most often, the first impression a customer gets of the firm. However, if the salespeople don't have a strong support team to intake, manage, and handle their generated sales, the system will break down, and your firm will end up with an unhappy customer.

In theory, everybody in the company is part of the sales team. As a leader, you cannot view just your salespeople as superheroes; you have to value the entire organization. Look at it this way: Your general contractor is the face of the project, but if the workers and subcontractors don't show up or do a good job, the project will fall apart quickly.

It is therefore critical to view everyone at your company as equals. Employees in different roles see different things and can solve many inefficiencies, thus improving the overall customer experience. Here are some recommended ways to get everybody on board:

- Conduct town hall meetings monthly. Prepare an agenda of issues the company is facing, and ask for guidance from the entire organization.

- Set individual meetings with support staff monthly to discuss processes, issues, and ideas to enhance the customer experience.

- Speak to your salespeople to see how the support teams are performing, and get recommendations and ideas from them.

- When rolling out contests or programs in the organization, be extremely mindful of including the entire company—no matter how difficult.

When you initiate a contest for your salespeople to increase sales and it is effective, additional work falls on the support team. It's critical that you remain mindful of this and attach a different reward or recognition for their efforts. Start looking at your company from a bird's-eye view, and recognize that all the parts must work well in tandem to be wildly successful. Geese fly in a V for endurance and energy, honking to show support for the lead goose and to reassure the team that the speed is accurate. As a leader, you need to get on board with this thinking by setting the speed of the company and maintaining it across all departments. How great would it be if you could empower your salespeople to honk every time they were assisted by the support teams?

My mom used to laugh at me when I took her shopping. She laughed because I had the ability to bring out someone's best characteristics by engaging directly with them. I created an experience wherever I went, not only for me but also for the people I came into contact with. I still do this today with intention; it just comes naturally to me. People appreciate and value a personal touch. People appreciate kindness. Perhaps I want to showcase and build the strengths I have available to me.

I also learned at a young age that you are less likely to get caught in the crossfire if you are respectful. So, I grew up being extremely respectful, which turned into being extremely pleasant.

As I got older, I valued engaging with people, and it became a fun challenge for the few who were extra grumpy or downright uninterested. I look at it this way: If I have to go out and do a bunch of errands on a Saturday, I might as well improve my service level and get the most out of it. So, I engage people. I *always* call people by their name, greet them, ask them how they are, ask them how their day is going, and compliment them for their service if it is good—and especially if it is superior.

Do you know what happens when you offer this kind of service to a service person? When I go to Dunkin' Donuts, I have a pre-made coffee just the way I like it handed to me ahead of eight other people in line. During the holiday rush, a Walmart cashier will open up a brand-new checkout line just for me. Countless experiences like this happen to me all the time. It's about subliminally telling people your needs and getting what you need in return. Rather than telling people what to do, it's about nudging them along, giving them the power and ownership to do what you would like them to do.

> *As a leader, rather than telling someone what to do, give them the power to discover it on their own.*

Growing Gratitude

Most everyone starts their day with a cup of coffee. Many of us have a bodega guy or a favorite barista we hope to see when we start our day. The small acts of kindness they deliver outside of the simple cup of coffee make us want to return and see them again and again. A dear friend of mine frequented the same coffee store every single morning in college. She would order the same breakfast sandwich and coffee each day from the same coffee lady. The day after her grandmother died, she walked past her favorite stop because she was too upset to visit. The coffee lady came running after her with her breakfast sandwich and coffee, recognizing that she was extremely upset. To this day, my dear friend has never forgotten that act of kindness—and the many others—she received with her morning coffee. Taking the time to show gratitude and appreciation is one of the most underutilized skills we have—and it's *free*!

Think about this: 81 percent of people say they would work harder for a grateful boss.[1] Yet, despite the evidence that all employees appreciate gratitude and recognition, 89 percent of bosses wrongly believe their employees quit because they want more money.[2]

So, how do you infuse gratitude into your daily work habits? It starts with being aware of your audience, your tone, the words you're using, and the body language you're displaying. Make it a point before you walk through your work doors in the morning to leave behind all that is going on at home. It is critical to separate and compartmentalize the two. Recognize that everyone has issues and problems; work should be the safe haven you create for an enjoyable, gratitude-filled culture. Here are some ways to impart gratitude into your daily culture and work habits:

- **Take a moment.** Greet your people, wish them a good morning, and offer a few words of coffee talk. Nobody likes it when work is thrown at them without a nod of acknowledgment.

- **Perform small acts of recognition.** Take a walk around the office and thank people for doing great work. Call out "stand out" moments! Visit departments that you generally would not frequent.

- **Spread the praise.** Verbal communication and recognition from the leader goes a long way. Enthusiasm and verbal praise instill a culture of reciprocity; if you are doing it, others will catch on and do it too!

- **Show altruistic appreciation.** Write a quick note (even a sticky) and put it on someone's desk. Buy coffee for a team when you go out to get yours. Note the little things that your employees love, and leave something special on their desk for them.

When you embody gratitude and infuse it into your daily culture, it becomes infectious, and everybody starts to model the same behaviors. These behaviors will have a trickle-down effect to your customers, preserving and maintaining your reputation.

The Three Vs

If you are lucky enough to meet a customer face-to-face these days, their impression of you begins the moment they step through your door—or even the moment they pull into your firm's parking lot. And since it takes sixty seconds or less to create an impression, you better be paying attention all the time.

Here are some incredible statistics about first impressions:

- Fifty-five percent of first impressions are made by what we see (visual).

- Thirty-eight percent are made by the way we hear your first words (vocal).

- Seven percent are made by the actual words you say (verbal).

- Research suggests that in *a tenth of a second*, people start determining traits like trustworthiness.[3]

Entrepreneurs see things through entrepreneurial lenses; they see things that others do not, which brings me to the three Vs:

1. **Visual:** body language and facial expressions

2. **Vocal:** the way in which you say things

3. **Verbal:** the words that you say

Each of these Vs has a profound impact on how people view you and your company.

Each morning when I arrived at work, I would take a walk around our building. I would notice garbage in the parking lot, a crooked banner, candy wrappers in the elevator, a burned-out lightbulb, empty business card holders, conference room chairs askew, dirty glasses in the conference rooms, and so on. I saw *everything* from miles away.

I used to think that most others saw these things too, but I have come to realize that is not the case. We were lucky enough to have a front desk administrator who cared deeply about our organization and the first impression our guests received when they entered our firm. She saw all the same things I did, and I was blessed to have her with me for twenty-plus years.

She always greeted our guests by name, was compassionate, and offered a warm smile, kind gestures, and recommendations, which immediately put all of our guests at ease. She used to literally jump out from behind her desk to offer them coffee or tea; then she would put them in a private meeting room and check on them routinely every five to ten minutes. She didn't just walk to greet our guests; she almost trotted to attend to them while displaying true attentiveness and consideration that few others offered.

As the old saying goes: "You don't get a second chance to make a good first impression."

According to one university study, people make eleven determinations about another person in the first seven seconds of contact ("The 7/11 Rule")[4]:

1. Education Level

2. Economic Level

3. Perceived Credibility, Believability, Competence, and Honesty

4. Trustworthiness

5. Level of Sophistication

6. Sex-Role Identification

7. Level of Success

8. Political Background

9. Religious Background

10. Ethnic Background

11. Social/Professional Desirability

And then, according to this study, the rest of their time is spent finding evidence to prove their original impression of that person, whether that impression is true or not.

Knowing all this, you can understand why it's so valuable to make a good first impression *and* to embody gratitude.

An Empathetic Ear

My company was in the business of getting people jobs, and for many, looking for a job can be a very upsetting and challenging time. We knew that many of these people were discouraged by their unemployed status and were having a hard time finding work, leaving some in a dire financial situation. Our firm needed to be a safe haven for them, a place that made them feel comfortable, where they could be honest and vulnerable so that we could help them.

I was extremely empathetic to their situations and was able to connect very effectively with them. Coming from the background that I did, I knew people had private issues and circumstances that drove their need for immediate work and stability. Who could relate to the need for stability more than me? That was something I understood intimately, coming as I did from such an unpredictable childhood.

Our employees were generally quite sensitive to these issues and knew the importance of greeting our anxious guests on time, armed with solutions to remedy their employment issues. Leaving an already anxious guest waiting only creates more anxiety, frustration, and defeat.

Every interaction in your company should evoke the same customer experience. When one of our staffing managers left a guest waiting, they were thwarting all the great work our receptionist had done to make a stellar first impression. Remember that everything you do represents and supports your sales and service process. You are creating experiences every day in many small, subtle ways, and you must be mindful of your work. Understand that you need the help of *all* your colleagues—from the parking attendant to the front desk administrator to the human resources assistant and up to the president and founder—to ensure your reputation remains untarnished. Much like a relay race, everyone shares responsibility for the outcome.

In many ways, I look at my childhood as a blessing, filled with many lessons I have come to value. I see people simply as people and make no judgments about their background or upbringing. When people meet me, they often assume I went to a prominent college and perhaps even have a master's degree. But I look at people through completely different lenses. I don't think about where they went to school or what degree they graduated with—I look at their behavioral skills, learn about their family and upbringing, and care to hear stories about how they grew up and what their life's principles are. As with a house, I like to wait and see what is underneath—a solid foundation or an unstable structure.

Remember: It is your company and your rules.

As a leader, you must create consistent patterns and policies and enforce those behaviors so your employees become trusted, accountable leaders.

When I opened the doors of McIntyre, I started the business with the mantra that we would treat people as we would hope to be treated. But a mantra is not enough—we needed to live by these values daily.

I worked tirelessly to ensure our firm provided exceptional service. Understand that your people crave guidance and structure and will want to follow a well-laid-out blueprint. I set consistent and measured policies to ensure that customers were greeted and met with quickly, that customers received routine follow-up calls within twenty-four hours, and that feedback to customers was provided within seventy-two hours. All these actions ensured an extremely high level of customer satisfaction at our firm.

These were just a few of the policies we implemented. You will find that if you don't have set policies that you monitor rigorously, your employees will happily create their own.

◻ PUNCH LIST

- -

- **Know that impressions matter.** Providing excellent service isn't a one-time event; it creates a lasting impression that will be long remembered.

- **Recognize that everyone contributes to sales.** Sales are important, but so is every other department, as everybody in the company is part of the sales team. Value them as such.

- **Take a bird's-eye view.** Examine your company from a bird's-eye view and pay attention to your employees' interactions.

- **Be reliable, be present, and be valuable.** Understand that each interaction you have with your customers is building trust and mutual respect.

- **Empower your people.** Rather than telling someone what to do, give them the power to discover it on their own. The lessons are likely to last longer.

- **Use the three Vs.** Remember to communicate using the three Vs: visual (body language and facial expressions); vocal (how you say things); and verbal (words you say).

- **Remember the 7/11 rule.** First impressions matter. People make eleven determinations about you in the first seven seconds of contact.

- **Use an empathetic ear.** Put yourself in another person's shoes. Give them a safe space and treat them with dignity. They'll remember.

Experience Chaos to Find Clarity

"Refuse to lower your standards to accommodate
those who refuse to raise theirs."

—MANDY HALE

I n the building industry, there are a lot of choices you can
make when you are buying products, and there are many
ways to cut costs. In truth, you will incur problems down the
road if you attempt to cut costs by downgrading to inferior-quality
products. As an example, there are at least eight different choices
for windows. You can buy the cheapest windows available, but
that will cut your window life expectancy in half, potentially invit-
ing water leaks and rot early on, which can end up costing you
well more than you saved in the first place. Or you can go with

a costlier window up front and come out ahead because they last twice as long and cause zero damage.

Whenever possible, you want to use the best products to build a strong, long-lasting structure.

> *When you build out your firm, create strong, sustainable processes and enforce them!*

I'll never forget the day it happened. It had already been a taxing month, and we were having a tough quarter; numbers were down, and we were working hard to get things back on track. After multiple interviews, we were still down a few salespeople, with no good prospects in sight. Things just weren't going our way. The labor pool was tight, which made recruiting that much more difficult, requiring extra diligence and scrutiny per candidate placement.

Additionally, the compensation for corporate recruiting positions was off the charts, making it exceedingly difficult to recruit talent into the staffing industry. I had just gotten out of a meeting with a few frustrated managers griping about the lack of talent, training issues—all the usual topics faced in businesses daily. Lots of problems thrown my way with no valuable solutions in sight.

Step Out of the Whirlwind

I was quickly running out to our coffee bar to grab something before my next meeting when I overheard the call. It was a rookie recruiter working in the office services team, debriefing a candidate after their first customer interview. Nothing cataclysmic, an innocent misstep—but the wrong work. She wasn't following our training protocol, which was a scripted debriefing asking the interviewee direct follow-up questions so we could gauge interest, excitement, next steps, the prevention of competitive offers, and so on.

The manager within earshot of the rookie clearly was not going to offer any training or guidance, leaving a valuable opportunity to coach and teach on the table. And I . . . I just kept walking. I was in my own whirlwind and too preoccupied with my own issues to stop and teach. I'll remember the moment for the rest of my years—not specifically the moment but the lesson and the negative effects of being in your own whirlwind.

Growing up, I remember plenty of whirlwind moments in our house. Plenty of teaching lessons were left on the table, but more importantly, plenty of opportunities were missed. My father inherited an extremely profitable plumbing business from my grandfather. My father was already a plumber, so this opportunity should have been a welcome and natural transition—something he could excel at. Sadly, he not only squandered that opportunity but also damaged the business so terribly he lost it completely a few years later. When you are afforded the opportunities to teach or make a situation better, you must not squander the chance. As a leader, you must be committed to keeping the bar high.

I was reminded of this lesson again at an Engage conference in Boston sponsored by Bullhorn, our ATS provider, and one of my dearest friends, Art Papas. I was sitting in the front row, as I was particularly excited to hear a four-star female general speak about her career. She was a compelling speaker and shared incredible stories about her family and moving up through the ranks in the army.

She spoke about a moment when she too was walking down the hall, late for a meeting, when a problem presented itself. A lieutenant was walking past her without his headgear. A soldier's professionalism is measured in part by his or her appearance, and proper wear of the military uniform is a matter of personal pride for all soldiers. In the army, a soldier must always carry their headgear—one of the many rules in the military. Of course, she immediately took notice. Although the thought of being late to her meeting almost caused her to walk right past that soldier, the general knew that no matter how small the correction, if she did not make it, she was automatically lowering the standards of the military.

She could easily have kept on walking to get to her meeting and the many pressing issues facing her that day—"her whirlwind." However, she pointed out that as leaders, every time we allow even the smallest of missteps to go unmentioned, we are automatically lowering our standards. An uncommon occurrence becomes a common occurrence and thus the new standard. The moment I heard her say those words, I reflected back on the times when minor lapses of process occurred in my own company, allowing erosion to begin.

> *When you allow for even the smallest error or omission to occur at your firm, you are slowly letting your company decline.*

After a long period of time, the damage gets worse until the entire process is gone, washed away. This is how key processes get eliminated at your firm. All of a sudden, that first-day trigger you created for new sales starts is no longer made, creating a gap in your process and losing you the opportunity to garner additional business. Not only was I allowing our bar to slowly deteriorate, but so were my managers. The director of one of our largest groups didn't see the value of making first-day check-in calls to our customers. That automatically eliminated the call to ask for additional business, which cost us the ability to generate 10–15 percent additional revenue each year.

From something as small as the way the phone is answered to something as large as culture, you must never allow the standards of your firm to become compromised. If you do, over time, the entire process will break down, and you will no longer own the firm you thought you owned. Business will get sacrificed, sales will decline, and processes will diminish and potentially be lost forever.

I've reflected on the many times I walked through the halls of my company and heard many of these minor infractions—a staff member not using our full company name when answering the phone, or someone forgetting to escort one of our guests to the elevator, leaving them to roam the hallways at our firm. Addressing these small yet important nuances made us the successful, recognized firm that we were.

Put the Reason behind the Request

Here is where you may go wrong. Not only is it critical to step out of the whirlwind and address these small, subtle, important issues, but it's also critical to give the "why." Putting the reason behind the request will grant a much greater return on your employee investments. Explain the reason behind the rule—its purpose. Owners have the ability to look ahead and envision what these tiny cracks and infractions can lead to.

Employees don't necessarily see things this way, and they need to be shown examples. Owners can easily see that a decline in a product's value can lead to a decline in revenue, which can then bring a potential layoff to a particular division. These are obvious problems entrepreneurs and owners recognize that employees might not see.

You owe it to your staff to do the right thing and make the corrections. Where I believe owners often fail in this area is in their *delivery* when providing feedback.

Back to that conference: The general stopped the soldier, and without reprimand or condescension, she reminded him of what an honor it is to serve our country and *why* he should always travel with his hands by his side holding his headgear. Messaging, communication, and delivery are critical in everything you do. You have to take the time to deliver the right message not only to your customers but to your employees too. Give the reason behind the request, but make sure to communicate what will ultimately happen if the request isn't followed.

Cautious Confrontation

Why are leaders and managers reluctant to critique and provide guidance to their employees? Most often, it is because people shy away from confrontation—and the very word *confrontation* sounds mean and scary. But it doesn't have to be.

Helping your people see things from the perspective of a leader will teach them valuable lessons and give them the tools they need to succeed.

Here are some tips on critiquing and coaching people to success:

- **Mind your tone.** It is extremely important as a leader to manage your emotions and remain calm and collected, regardless of how dire the circumstances might be. Be clear with your message, take the time to spell out the issue, and provide the correct remedy. Before finishing your conversation, always circle back and have the recipient recap the conversation to ensure you are both aligned.

- **Be careful when correcting someone in front of a group.** Oftentimes a situation will transpire in a meeting or group setting when critiquing is necessary. Correcting someone in a group setting is convenient and can allow other people to receive the message you want to convey, and it can be a good opportunity for training. But it can also be difficult because some of your employees might be thicker-skinned than others. Be extremely self-aware, and carefully measure and frame how you are going to correct this person in a group setting. Knowing your people is very important when providing correction. If they are extremely fragile or emotional, you might want to consider speaking with them privately. I will dive further into this in a later chapter.

Paint a picture for your colleagues of how these small infractions can add up to tremendous long-term damage to the business. Use the lesson to instill pride, making someone want to do their best work. Don't leave them with a feeling of disappointment or embarrassment. How you deliver the message to your employees is critical, not only for how you are viewed as a leader but for how they receive your message.

About a year after hearing the general speak, I was back in Boston for the Engage Staffing conference sponsored by Bullhorn, the largest ATS/CRM software provider for staffing firms. I was a VIP attendee that year because Art Papas, the founder of Bullhorn, asked me to attend. I had been his very first customer, and our relationship started in 1999. The minute I met Art and he introduced his brand-new company to me, I knew that with him leading the charge, it would be a huge success in the staffing space. The idea was brilliant, the timing of the technology was perfect, and Art—well, he is one of the best people I've ever met: brilliant, humble, kind, and truly a leader people would follow anywhere.

The firm experienced phenomenal success and continues to own the ATS market for the staffing industry to this day. Art's keynote was a very vulnerable discussion about how he lost sight of his customers and the process of serving. The firm was growing by leaps and bounds (50 percent year over year) but was no longer putting the customer first. At that time, their internal mantra was "global domination." Everyone in the company was focused on growth—but not on the customer experience. Art had stopped looking at their NPS (Net Promoter Score), the key indicator from their customers on their performance. He was so busy keeping up with the growth he had stopped looking. And when he finally did look, he found that he was at a -50 NPS!

It happens to the best of us: We get so wrapped up in the growth—or the challenges, people problems, missed forecasts, and so on—that we lose sight of the very things that made us successful to begin with. Art had gotten caught up in driving growth and momentarily forgot the customer experience. I was a VIP guest because I was the customer who told him candidly that he had a big problem. After almost twenty years of service together, I was leaving the relationship—and I was Art's first customer and biggest fan!

But that year, they hit a crossroads, and Art became acutely aware they had a problem that needed fixing. I'll never forget the call I made to Art telling him that we would be leaving him as a customer. I was sick to my stomach and couldn't imagine not working with our best and most valued partner ever again. I took my vendor relationships very seriously, rarely changing the firms that dedicated their time, hard work, and solutions to support our firm's growth. This one was my strongest and longest relationship. They were also the firm that I took great pride in referring—to the point of almost being pushy. I was a customer ambassador by choice, quite insistent that other staffing firms who were not using their services should— as they offered such a robust solution to talent management.

Art listened, self-reflected, and made some hard decisions, diagnosing what was going wrong culturally at Bullhorn. What Art did next was what few people can or will do—he changed everything. He put the customer first again and changed all the company values to focus their employees on service first. He hammered home the importance of valuing their customer relationships. He centered *everything* around the customer—and the company started to change. Art was able to step out of the whirlwind, digest, analyze what had gone wrong, and humbly implement strategies to immediately rectify the situation.

Few leaders have the ability to recognize when they have a big problem, let alone make the effort to remedy it. Yet Art did, and he chose to be vulnerable and honest on stage in front of most of his customers, colleagues, and friends. Most importantly, Art was open enough to listen to what I had to say and humble enough to ask me for patience while he began the journey to repair his firm's customer relations.

Today Bullhorn is a $300 million firm and still growing, from start-up to software giant. They continue to be the leader in their field, and Art remains in charge today as the CEO and cofounder. Their NPS Score is +50, a significant change in opinion from the very same customers—and not one Bullhorn employee would dare whisper those two words "global domination" ever again.

Customer-Centric Cycle

When you step out of the whirlwind to invest in your people and groom them to be brand ambassadors—living and breathing your services and products every day—you are not only developing your crew but also naturally cultivating stronger customer relationships. You are being so customer-centric that your customers will start selling your services for you too, bragging about your brand as much as your employees do. This goes right back to the theory we discussed in Lesson 5: Construct the Frame, where we introduced the "brag behind the brand."

⌂ PUNCH LIST

- -

- **Step out of your whirlwind.** Don't miss opportunities to correct and bolster your staff.

- **Recognize that small things add up.** When you let the smallest error stand, you begin a slow decline, as this behavior becomes accepted across the firm.

- **Address issues head-on.** Don't squander opportunities for training and learning.

- **Share the reason behind the request.** When we are afforded opportunities to teach or make a situation better, share the reason behind the request. Explain what will happen if the behavior doesn't change.

- **Don't lower the bar.** Again, consistency counts. From things as small as the way the phone is answered to something as large as culture, don't allow the standards of your firm to become compromised.

- **Remain customer-centric.** Your customers will start selling your services for you—another version of the "brag behind the brand."

PART 4

Budgeting

Having and following a budget is critical to the success and development of your business. Much like a blueprint, a budget is your road map—a tool you should refer back to often to ensure that you're on track with your forecasts, maintaining a steady pace, and not overextending the company. A budget is critical when you are building or renovating, as it is quite easy to go over budget with only one or two small change orders.

Additionally, both in building and business, there are always hidden surprises. A well-managed and seasoned business will put quite a bit of cash aside so that *when*—not *if*—a crisis or issue occurs, they will be prepared. When budgeting, it is important to look ahead at the entire scope of a project to decide which areas are most important to shift money into.

But budgets don't just apply to numbers; they also apply to pipelining and customer engagement. Someone who is responsible for revenue growth must budget their time to ensure they reach and engage with potential customers. I found that many of my staff spent a great deal of time procrastinating when it came to speaking with customers rather than budgeting their time for maximum results.

Measure Only
What Matters

"Too much data can be a death sentence."

—CHARLES FIRLOTTE

I n the building industry, there is a familiar saying: "Measure twice, cut once." Be thorough and eliminate mistakes. But more importantly, be exacting and measure carefully first. When you're building something, it's extremely important to get the measurements right. An eighth of an inch can throw a whole project off. In business, you need to look at measurements and analyze what is important to investigate to help your firm thrive and grow.

Starting work at such a young age, I took great pride in and ownership of my work. Even the most menial task was extremely important to me. Perhaps it reflected my personal brand. I wanted to enhance my character and build my reputation, and quality of work was something I genuinely cared about. Since I did not have a great family foundation, pride in my work was one thing that was within my control.

Every business should have measurements. KPIs are used to measure many aspects of your business, including outcomes and the progress of projects. Having a dashboard of KPIs is vital to your business, as these outcomes are the net results of your work. KPIs are a great way to measure what is going on in your business in a non-emotional manner, putting the focus on only the actual outcome, creating a consistent way to manage your business over time. How do you decide what KPIs are best for your firm? This is a highly personal decision and should be well thought out and discussed.

KPIs are like adopting a successful health-and-wellness program. There are plenty to choose from and many iterations; only you know what is best for you. To diagnose and define your KPIs, consider "The Onion Exercise," a six-step approach to uncover key metrics.

Start broad and peel back the layers to uncover results.

Peel Back the Onion

THE ONION EXERCISE

Think Big
Narrow the Scope
Talk It Out
Prioritize & Refine
Measure & Monitor
Share KPIs

1. **Think big.** Revenue—Growth—Company Goals—Verticals—Customer Retention Rate. For a C-level executive, an overarching goal might be to increase sales revenue by 15 percent by end of year. A manager responsible for a division might set their sights on quarterly growth of 5 percent. To get the KPIs that suit you best, I recommend you slowly peel back the onion.

2. **Narrow the scope.** What sales objectives will get you to your goals? What is your average customer spend? What are your total monthly sales? What is your gross profit? It's important to keep this information relative to your business and industry.

3. **Talk it out.** Start vetting the goals and numbers. Look at what work needs to be done to achieve these goals. How much additional business do you need to achieve from how many customers to get to X monthly sales? Look at your sales pipeline: How many opportunities are needed? How many opportunities can be turned into wins? How many proposals need to be sent out? How many meetings need to be scheduled?

4. **Prioritize and refine.** Gather your key metrics and reduce them to five to eight key performance items. You want the most critical data that will drive your company forward. Measure only what truly matters.

5. **Measure and monitor.** It's important to measure KPIs consistently and over time. Allow data collection quarter by quarter before basing long-term decisions on this data. It is also okay to change a KPI if it is not proving important. (Just be certain you have given it a sufficient amount of time.)

6. **Share KPIs with the company.** It is important to be transparent with your KPIs and share them with your people. Having open and honest communication around your KPIs—and the company's performance—will foster ideas, progress, and good outcomes. It's essential that all your employees are aware of the company goals and objectives so they can work toward them and provide feedback as necessary.

Try It—Before You Buy It

Now that you have created your five to eight KPIs, the first thing you need to do is get buy-in and support from your employees and adoption from your leaders. You want your leaders to be comfortable with the KPIs that have been chosen, most of which hopefully came directly from them. Without adoption from the managers, the process will be inconsistent and inconclusive. If you don't get buy-in from the employees, behaviors won't change, and their performance may decline, meaning your efforts will have been for nothing. Spend time meeting with your management team to ensure you have complete alignment and commitment prior to rolling out these KPIs.

Second, make sure the numbers you report are correct. If there is a possibility the numbers aren't accurate or are inaccurately sourced, you will create doubt. Once doubt sets in, you will lose support for this process, and negative behaviors may follow.

One by one, your employees will start to question the validity of the numbers and have discussions among themselves. Once this happens, doubt and frustration will set in, and all the work you have done will become worthless. Your employees will believe the process isn't important because it's not accurate; some might even stop reporting their numbers altogether. This will become a very negative experience, and your staff will lose faith.

When we initially started the adoption process for our KPIs, our CRM system was not accurately reporting the results. This threw my salespeople into a tailspin. They started digging into all the KPIs versus the CRM results. It created a lot of undue frustration, time loss, and doubt. I highly recommend that prior to adoption, you perform several tests to ensure that all the numbers and results are properly reported. If you don't do this, your staff might continue to doubt the overall process, leaving you with a failed implementation of something extremely valuable to your company's growth.

Someone needs to champion this process and ensure that it is managed correctly and that the numbers are being sourced properly. You and your leaders must take your time, work with your technical team, and make sure you are reporting and adopting the right KPIs and that everyone is in full agreement. Think about core processes, and discuss what you really want to measure. Test drive your KPIs for a few months to work out the kinks before you roll them out to your people.

Third, you must spend a good amount of time evaluating the numbers. You can't just jump to conclusions if you have one negative month or one positive month. Take at least two quarters' worth of data to analyze and review. The more time you invest in your KPIs, the more telling and valuable the data will become. Also, make sure you have chosen the right KPIs and that everyone agrees with them. You do not want to fight about the numbers. If you manage this incorrectly, your people will spend more time reviewing and refuting the numbers than actually making the improvements the numbers suggest are needed.

Fourth, when creating the metrics, decide how you will handle downturns and what actions will be carried out if those low numbers persist. People will be holding their breath in anticipation—waiting for a bad number to come out, altering the numbers, or spending a significant amount of time defending the numbers (and not selling). It is simply good management to plan for outcomes ahead of time, and it will allow your people time to adopt and become comfortable.

As you gather and review the data from your KPIs, you will start to see areas that are worth investing in or eliminating. If you find that you have been investing $10,000 a quarter in elaborate marketing campaigns that have yielded minimal results, you might want to pivot and try something different with that money. When you do that, you can create a new KPI to monitor this new action. Analyzing and digesting the results are extremely important for successful outcomes.

Be S.M.A.R.T.

Whenever you are creating goals for your company, you want to keep the acronym S.M.A.R.T. in mind.[1]

S = SPECIFIC—Make your goals specific for effective planning.

M = MEASURABLE—Define what evidence will prove you're making progress, and reevaluate when necessary.

A = ATTAINABLE—Make sure you can attain your goal in a reasonable amount of time.

R = RELEVANT—Ensure that your goals align with your values and long-term objectives.

T = TIME BASED—Set a realistic, ambitious end date for task prioritization and motivation.

Bite-Sized Goals

The Goals Blueprint is an outline that will help you map out one "bite-sized" specific goal at a time, building out the tactics and strategies needed for success. It will also show you short-term results on what works and what doesn't. When one of your managers is struggling with an issue or challenge, this worksheet will help them map out the problem and solution. Perhaps one of the initiatives in your organization is to grow a vertical 20 percent. The Goals Blueprint will help you set the goal, develop a clear objective, create strategies and tactics to drive results, and measure effectiveness from the results.

GOALS BLUEPRINT

GOAL Example: • Increase revenue 20%	
OBJECTIVES Example: • Attract ten new customers in XXX time	
STRATEGIES Example: • Increase # of new prospective leads • Increase call conversation rate • Add XXX followers to social site(s) • Convert quotes received to sales	
TACTICS Example: • Advertising Google AdWords • Partner with XXX—Who can you align/partner with to grow business? • Garner three customer testimonials based on "Ideal Customer" profile • Launch new member blog • Hold monthly loyalty events/seminars • Create private Facebook group for members	

MEASUREMENTS/ROI (MEASURE WHAT MATTERS)	
Example: • # of Google leads • # of local partnership referrals • % of conversions using testimonials • # of new members • # of blog visits • # of website downloads • # of events • # of Facebook group members—retention rate	

When working in the remodeling field, I found it was imperative to review the different prices I was given and dissect each of them for content. Oftentimes, a conversation with the foreman would reveal that there were a few different ways a project could get done. Discussing options and getting everybody on board with the numbers are vital to the growth and consistency of your business.

⌂ PUNCH LIST

- -

- **Rely on the numbers.** Create a dashboard of KPIs, and monitor these numbers consistently.

- **Apply the Onion Method.** To diagnose and define your KPIs, consider "The Onion Exercise," a six-step approach to uncover key metrics.

- **Create S.M.A.R.T. goals.** Choose five to eight KPIs. Make them specific, measurable, attainable, relevant, and time-based. Measure only what truly matters.

- **Follow your Goals Blueprint.** Determine and set goals using a systematic strategy.

- **Create alignment.** Spend time meeting with your management team to ensure that you have complete alignment and commitment prior to rolling out these KPIs.

- **Set bite-sized goals.** When setting a goal, use the Goal Blueprint to map out your tactics and strategies for best results.

Make Time for Restoration

"One reason so few of us achieve what we truly want is
that we never direct our focus; we never concentrate on power.
Most people dabble their way through life,
never deciding to master anything in particular."

—TONY ROBBINS

General contractors who manage a crew oversee all the work. Generally, they don't do the actual work, but they are constantly managing the flow of labor, while other tradespeople are the executors for the project. The contractors spearhead the whole project and are responsible for each deadline and the overall outcome. They arrive at the site each morning, discuss the plan and vision for the day, leave the crew to do the work, and return at day's end. They work "on" the business rather than "in" the business.

In your own business, it is critical to step away from the business, clear your head, participate in other avenues—training, idea sharing—and invest in yourself so that you can be a strong leader.

Make a Meeting with Yourself

Some high-end executive coaches insist that their customers remove themselves from the business for a set period of time each week. In this way, leaders can clear their minds, focus on new ideas, and create clarity for future opportunities. As a leader, you should create a set meeting with yourself each week, ensuring that you are consistent with scheduling. This is something you can easily remove from your calendar but is critical to the focus, growth, and development of you and your company.

A survey by Manchester Inc. of one hundred executives found that coaching provided an average return on investment of almost six times the cost of the coaching.[1] Spending time outside of the business—networking or attending events—even briefly, is essential to the growth of your firm. Many successful entrepreneurs will tell you that they block off a window of time weekly to simply think about the business, ruminate on new ideas, and solve critical issues.

As a leader, I always had to be "on." Oftentimes, I found that always being "on" prevented me from thinking about things on a deeper level; it stalled my learning and the spark for the best ideas. Frequently, I would impulsively share the first thing that came to mind rather than doing a deep dive on an issue or even spending a few hours to think about something more fully. Due to the nature of our business, a fast response was often required, but it didn't always produce the best result. You cannot just be a knowledge learner; you have to be a learning worker. Learning requires stepping out of the day-to-day business for recharging and reflection, not constant action.

The poster child for this idea is Thomas J. Watson Jr., the long-time CEO of IBM, who built the company into a major global organization. The story goes that in 1911, when Watson was in a meeting with sales managers at National Cash Register, he became frustrated by the lack of good ideas among the attendees. "The trouble with every one of us is that we don't think enough," he declared. "Knowledge is the result of thought, and thought is the keynote of success in this business or any business."[2]

The case for contemplation is powerful, yet most of us don't include practicing reflection and relaxation in our professional tool kit. We have a bias for busyness, and it keeps us from pausing to learn.

It's Lonely at the Top

Being an entrepreneur can be isolating, lonely, and frustrating, leaving you with few people to talk to. People who share common problems and issues are skilled at providing sound solutions in a matter of moments. They also help you resolve future issues: when to implement new processes and systems, strategies to manage and grow your staff, ways to improve culture—the ideas and issues are endless. Getting outside feedback from like-minded entrepreneurs and peers is vital to the success and growth of your company, but even more important is finding the time to do so.

Time is something everyone wants more of. It's something I could never seem to find enough of when I owned my staffing firm. And it's something you are going to struggle with a lot as an entrepreneur. Managing and prioritizing your time is extremely important, and you will need to get very good at it. The average person uses thirteen different methods to control and manage their time. The average person gets one interruption every eight minutes, or approximately seven times an hour, or fifty to sixty times per day. The average interruption takes five minutes, totaling about four hours, or 50 percent of the average workday.[3]

In the early days, my management team did not see the value of investing in outside educational seminars or conferences, citing lack of time. They constantly stayed at their desks, telling me they simply were too busy to attend these events. Not seeing the value in stepping away, networking with peers, and learning new things is shortsighted. Some remarkable changes in my business stemmed from ideas and takeaways at these conferences. An internal report of the Personnel Management Association showed that when training is combined with coaching, individuals increase their productivity by an average of 86 percent compared to 22 percent with training alone.[4] Did you know that almost all the Fortune 100 leaders have a private coach? A Hay Group study found that 40 percent of executives utilize a coach, and coaching is a standard for leadership development for elite executives.[5]

The staffing industry has a tremendous amount of support, such as the ASA—the American Staffing Association—a large association in Washington, DC. I would often rely on their well-seasoned staff, who were readily armed to help me with just about anything I needed. They offered annual conferences, webinars, and even templates for our industry, and they also lobbied for our rights. But I recommend that you attend more than just industry-specific conferences; do additional research. I found that I got my best ideas at marketing conferences and from reading about how market conditions are vastly changing.

Most importantly, familiarize yourself with organizations that are larger than yours, and utilize their resources. They have already taken the next steps and have made the leap to the next revenue marker. They will have most of the answers to the challenges you are currently struggling with.

Put Time on Your Side

Entrepreneurs are generally hard-chargers—they think they are made of Teflon and can outwork most other people. But this kind of behavior is old-school thinking and has become antiquated. You always need to be at your best performance level to lead your people.

I used to have an employee who, when asked, "How are you?" would always respond with "I'm so busy." It's beneficial to change that answer for two reasons. One: Telling someone you are busy is off-putting, especially if they are coming to you for help. Two: "Busy is the new stupid," or so says Bill Gates. Instead, focus on working smarter and more efficiently. If you can learn to manage your time better, you will get more accomplished in fewer hours, leaving time to enjoy outside activities and your personal life. This boils down to tight time management, discipline, and following a consistent plan. If you show your employees how to maximize their time at work, focusing on prioritization, they'll be able to manage their workday much more efficiently, creating more time for outside interests.

You must value time management and time off to rejuvenate so you can be your best self.

Here are a few statistics on time management that were surprising to me:

Up to 80 percent of the average working day is spent on activities with little or no value. This means that most people only spend 20 percent of their working day on tasks considered important.

1. Managers spend as many as three hours per working day dealing with interruptions.[6]

2. Business owners spend up to seven hours a week on wasted activities.[7]

3. People who set goals are ten times more likely to succeed than those who don't.[8]

4. Senior managers spend twenty-three hours per week in meetings.[9]

5. The average employee spends two hours and eleven minutes procrastinating each day, often by doing the following:

   - Texting—up to twenty-eight minutes
   - Daydreaming—up to twenty minutes
   - Gossiping—up to eighteen minutes
   - Going on Facebook—up to sixteen minutes[10]

Here is a method I used to create a more efficient time-management system for myself and my company leaders.

4 Es of Time Management

1. **EXECUTE.** Important enough to go on the top of your priority list.

2. **ENTRUST.** Important and needs priority but not yours. Entrust it to a leader at your firm.

3. **ENVELOPE.** Seal it, date it, and defer it to a future month.

4. **ELIMINATE.** Not worth anyone's time. Scrap it.

Take your never-ending to-do list and run it through these four categories. **Eliminate** what isn't important, **Entrust** what is important to a capable colleague, and **Envelope** what you can defer to a later date. Your list is now left with only items that you personally need to **Execute** on. This is a simple exercise that should be performed weekly. It will help you improve your time management and allow you more time to do what you do best, which is lead, innovate, and work "on" the business.

Here is a simple worksheet to help you with your 4 Es:

THE FOUR Es OF TIME MANAGEMENT

EXECUTE

(Important enough to go on the top of your priority list)

❑ _____
❑ _____
❑ _____
❑ _____
❑ _____
❑ _____
❑ _____
❑ _____
❑ _____

ENTRUST

(Important and needs priority but not yours. Entrust it to a leader at your firm.)

❑ _____
❑ _____
❑ _____
❑ _____
❑ _____
❑ _____
❑ _____
❑ _____
❑ _____

ENVELOPE

(Seal it, date it, and defer it to a future month.)

❑ _____
❑ _____
❑ _____
❑ _____
❑ _____
❑ _____
❑ _____
❑ _____
❑ _____

ELIMINATE

(Not worth anyone's time—scrap it!)

❑ _____
❑ _____
❑ _____
❑ _____
❑ _____
❑ _____
❑ _____
❑ _____
❑ _____

Active Distractions

If you are still convinced that you simply cannot leave your business, find some way to decompress and clear your head. Go for a walk, run, or drive; listen to a podcast; or read a trade magazine, a business book, or the local paper. I found several podcasts that were industry-specific, helpful, and refreshing, always providing one or two valuable takeaways. I would break at lunch to work out in our company gym because I found that some of my best ideas came when I was on a treadmill, just taking time to clear my mind and create active distractions.

Research and reading are also critically important. Perhaps there are not webinars or seminars to go to—find some books that can help guide you. When I was young, I turned to books. Not only was reading a wonderful escape for me, but books were my teachers. You can gather little nuggets or completely change an internal process based on some of the material that is available today.

You need to find quiet time to clear your mind so that new ideas and answers can come to you. In my monthly forum, I noticed most of the members followed these best practices, and the most successful leaders scheduled time weekly to sit quietly and "think." Once again, I thought, *Who has time for this?* until I finally realized that these are best practices followed by some of the most powerful and successful leaders today.

Did you know that many successful leaders spend time doing daily meditation and schedule time weekly to sit quietly and reflect on their business—to simply think? By 2022, the value of the US meditation market will be a bit over $2 billion. Fifty-two percent of employers provided mindfulness classes or training to their employees in 2018.[11] The benefits employees reported for meditation were overwhelmingly positive:

- Improves general wellness—76.2 percent

- Improves energy—60 percent

- Aids memory and concentration—50 percent

- Reduces anxiety—29.2 percent

- Reduces stress—21.6 percent

- Reduces depression—17.8 percent[12]

One of my most highly regarded entrepreneur friends meditates every morning for twenty minutes. He runs a $150 million successful business in Connecticut. When I spoke with him about his meditation practices, he said that it truly enhances his leadership qualities. He finds that he is extremely calm, levelheaded, and focused for the day after his twenty-minute morning session. I would also note that he has an extremely high level of gratitude and empathy.

With all the stress, crisis management, and decision-making involved in being an entrepreneur, you need to establish some healthy outlets to feed your soul, body, and mind. It is necessary to step out of the weeds, get away from your business, spend time with like-minded leaders, take care of yourself, and invest in the vision and growth of your business. You and only you can create the vision for tomorrow, as it is no longer enough to be good—in today's competitive landscape, you have to be great!

Find ways to improve your time-management skills and schedule blocks of time just for you. See the value and importance of investing in yourself, and teach your staff about time management, balancing work and play, and working more efficiently and productively so they can enjoy their time off and personal activities.

As a leader, you must establish healthy ways in which to conduct and manage your work because you are in this for the long haul.

⌂ PUNCH LIST

- -

- **Make a meeting with yourself.** Set aside time away from the business every week. This allows you to clear your mind, focus on new ideas, and create clarity for future opportunities.

- **Be willing to learn.** We cannot just be knowledge learners; we must be learning workers.

- **Be disciplined with time.** Implementing time management is vital to ensuring a productive workday.

- **Implement the 4 Es.** Eliminate what isn't important, Entrust what's important to capable colleagues, Envelope what you can defer to a later date, and then Execute on what remains.

- **Enhance personal productivity.** Consider hiring an executive coach; most leaders in the Fortune 100 rely on them. Expect your productivity to increase.

- **Mind your mental state.** Meditation is an effective way to unplug, focus, and prepare for your day or recharge in the middle of a busy day.

PART 5

Demolition

Demolition is a critical part of the construction business. It's fast and furious but can often uncover something you never even knew was there. It is a period where contractor and homeowner hold their breath, knowing all too well that there could be something very costly underneath all that sheetrock and lumber. And once you uncover it, you must own it—and make an important decision on how to repair it. You must repair damage to mitigate further damage before it either becomes too costly or potentially irreparable.

There will come a time when you must do demolition within your own business. You might have to deconstruct an entire team, remove an employee that is damaging your culture, or upgrade your B- and C-level employees to A-level players. If you stay true to your blueprint, you might have to take a department back to its timbers so that you can stay aligned with your mission.

Salvage What's Valuable

"Make sure everybody in your 'boat' is rowing and
not drilling holes when you're not looking."

—BRUCE LEWIS

There are some bad builders out there and many that can shortcut a project. Whenever you are remodeling, you are bound to find rotted wood, damage from old water leaks, insect and rodent damage, or simply eroding products that need to be replaced. I have seen damage so bad that it has altered the foundation of a house. One must mitigate such damage quickly by either cutting out all the dead rot or completely replacing the wood and starting over with fresh product. Initially, it might cut into your budget to replace the eroded materials with new, but in the end, it will yield the best result and long-term benefits.

Because of the nature of our corporate staffing and recruiting business, we functioned in separate divisions that offered specialized staffing services. It wouldn't make sense for an information technology recruiter to look for an accounting candidate and vice versa. These verticals needed to work together as a team when partnering on shared customer accounts, but they needed to work individually when representing their specific industry sector.

When I was younger, I started a job in the paper division of a communications company, working my way up from the bottom. My job was to type up all inbound orders that we took over the phone onto five-ply requisition forms and ensure the orders went out on time. The position afforded me the opportunity to see how people worked, what customers liked, and what behaviors they appreciated. I also saw gaps in our sales process and areas where improvements could be made.

I loved this job and took it very seriously. So when I noticed a flaw in the ordering process very early on, I took action. The same customers called weekly for one or two rolls of paper. This seemed very inefficient, and I thought of a better way. When these customers called me, I started to upsell them cases of paper instead of rolls. After a conversation with the shipping foreman at our company, I was able to show these customers that they would save money not only per roll but on overall shipping costs. After a period of time, cases turned into skids of paper, then multiple skids for larger customers. More customers started to request me when they called—much to the chagrin of my colleague at the desk next to me—and the revenue I was generating increased substantially, as did the irritation of that colleague.

Every night at five-thirty, I would ensure that my inbox holding open orders was empty, yet my colleague's was not. When I questioned her about preparing the final orders of the day to get them to the plant before our last shipment went out at six, she would dismiss my idea and say that the customers' shipments could wait until tomorrow. This lack of care surprised and frustrated me, as we had an obligation to our company and customers to display superior customer service.

Slow Rot

When I think back on this job, I realize that this employee had the ability to change the behavior of colleagues she worked with. When I arrived, she had been with the company for over ten years and worked in a very slow and plodding fashion. Lucky for me, I didn't allow her behavior to rub off on me or hinder my job performance and service to the customer in any way. But what would have happened if a person with a different work ethic had come into this role? Her rot would have slowly infected this person, and the customer experience and revenue of the company would have faltered.

She did not like what I was doing and thought I was showing her up. We were the only two people in the department, and we sat side by side. This was a dilemma for me. Yet my customers were extremely valuable, and I took great pride in my work. I knew I was doing the right work, which meant I was valuable to my company and its customers. I told my colleague that I would be happy to show her how I was increasing my revenue and making my customers happy, but she was not interested. So I carried on doing what I felt was best for our customers.

The Upsell

Soon after, I discovered another way to make money for the company. I sought out companies that were not buying from our firm but were using similar products. I used some of my existing customers as testimonials and started to earn new business with these customers. Long story short, I increased business so significantly that the warehouse had to hire two additional people.

Since I was now shipping skids and skids of paper out to new customers daily, I also had to ensure my products were being delivered properly and arriving on time. I made a point of fostering a close relationship with all the warehouse employees, especially the foreman. Quite often, I arrived early in the morning, when the warehouse was quiet and the workers were enjoying their morning coffee. Armed with several boxes of donuts, I would spend thirty minutes with the warehouse people discussing the daily shipments and ensuring my skids got priority treatment.

This extra effort and attention to detail afforded me the opportunity for advancement in the firm. I was ultimately promoted to manager of inside sales, where I built a team of four people doing exactly what I was doing: upselling to existing customers, establishing new customers, and ensuring customer satisfaction. I loved this job and still remember it fondly today, as it afforded me incredible learning opportunities. I was able to remediate issues and inefficient processes, which gave me the opportunity to better serve the customer. That is what it is all about: serving the customer!

At my staffing company, we always had a strong culture because we laid the proper foundation from the beginning. We had a strong team of united people who generally liked one another. We were fortunate enough to be able to give Rolex watches to our employees on their ten-year anniversaries and brand-new cars to several of our employees on their twenty-year anniversary. We celebrated our people with trips to Italy and the Caribbean and had all sorts of great parties, contests, and anniversary celebrations.

However, even with the strongest culture, now and then, a problematic employee can cause erosion. The erosion can start out small, so small you might not detect it right away.

Years ago, one of my customers, a large spirits company, came
to me with two job opportunities
in the accounting area. They were
a very good customer of ours—our
partnership had spanned more than

> *The problem is that rot spreads quickly and infects other people in the company.*

ten years. When vetting the job openings, I asked my contact, the
senior human resources manager, why these two positions were
coming available. I was hoping to hear they'd opened up due to a
promotion, so I could showcase a career trajectory for my potential
candidates, but both positions were open because of a personality
conflict with the accounting manager. That information sent a red
flag up for me, and I started to dig further.

What I found out was that this department of ten had been
cleared out completely over the last two years, and everyone had
been replaced except the manager! Oftentimes when there was an
issue of this magnitude, a customer would use several different
staffing firms to avoid damage to their reputation and get new
replacements in over and over. This was a very difficult situation to
be in. My sense of integrity demanded that I vet out our customers'
job opportunities carefully for the talent I represented, and I was
obligated to be honest with the customer and counsel them as best
I could for a successful outcome.

Clearly, this was something I didn't have to bring to my customer's attention. She was aware of the problem and did not know
what to do. She was extremely distraught and beside herself, so I
thought it best to meet face-to-face to discuss these issues further
before any action was taken.

After spending an hour with my customer, I convinced her to
take this matter to the CFO and remedy the problem. The cost of
replacing and training the entire department had already soared

over $100,000, and the department morale was terrible. This company is a marvelous brand, boasts a remarkable culture, and has a great reputation. Luckily, the problems were isolated primarily in this department, so removing the manager would solve the problem. The manager who was causing all the issues had to be dealt with. Because this was a confidential matter, I was not made aware of the finer details, but I do know that eventually they were able to terminate this manager for cause and hire a new one.

In the interim, I was able to place two strong-willed consultants in these open positions while the customer remedied the problem. My conversation with the two consultants prior to their start was honest and transparent. I made sure they knew the manager was a problem and action was being taken. I also instructed them to report any actions or situations that might occur to me directly and immediately. We closely managed the situation to ensure the consultants were working in a safe and professional environment, and soon after, the manager was terminated.

Offense vs. Defense

This situation turned out to have a very happy ending, but not before the company turned over an entire department of ten; spent over a year replacing competent, happy employees; spent months of human resource efforts to deal with these issues and openings; and incurred costs of over $100,000 to replace and train talent. To me, this issue was a non-emotional, easily solved problem. Had they remediated the obvious rot in the company and terminated the non-aligned employee earlier, it is likely none of these other bad things would have occurred.

Bear in mind, it is important to have your policies and procedures in order and aligned with your employee handbook. Prior to terminating any employee, your should consider all other remedies available to you. The mere fact that this employee did not align culturally with the company was the reason to start the documentation process. Oftentimes, when it is your own problem at your own company, the solutions do not seem quite as obvious as they do for those on the outside.

Permanent Damage

Have you ever had a slow leak? Drip, drip, drip. We had a slow water leak at the old house we'd renovated in Vermont. Drip, drip, drip. That slow leak caused a permanent stain on our shower floor that I would not have thought possible. My husband told me it was from the slow, consistent droplets of well water. Well water has a lot of minerals in it, and the minerals can stain porous materials.

We can also incur slow rot in our companies. This can happen through yes-men/women who seem to be adhering to your MVPs but really aren't. Obvious people-problems are easy to detect and remediate, but this subtle, slow rot is the real problem to look out for.

I had a director in our firm who was thought of as a very lovely person and quite liked by her team. She had been with me a long time and managed a team that was very strong, filled with tenured employees and loyal customers who had been with us for decades. Her job was to manage her team, manage existing business, acquire and drive new business, and ensure that our consultants were deployed safely and properly to our customers.

She did her job well because of her strong team but did not drive or acquire new business. I was the one who continually directed her on which customers to heavily manage and call. She did not have the business acumen to figure this out and was not sales-driven whatsoever. Because she was so well-liked, I thought she was culturally well suited for our firm, and I never spent too much time thinking about replacing her for a stronger candidate.

This was a mistake. She was a slow drip, a rot that worked its way through our firm and infected people in a very deliberate and methodical way.

She was a yes-woman—someone who smiled, always seemed cooperative, but was secretly talking behind our backs and drilling holes in our boat, trying to negatively influence as many people at the company as she could. Sadly, in this person's defense, I am not sure she fully knew that her actions would have such a negative impact. She ruined some really good employees and forced others out of the company with her subtle, negative ways.

I should have followed the advice I have given before: "You can only move the needle so far on someone."

People will make small changes, but you can never radically change someone unless they really want to change.

Making a lasting change in behavior is rarely a simple process. In 1980, James Prochaska discovered the five stages of change and labeled them the "readiness-to-change" model.[1] A person has to go through these five stages to truly change their thoughts and behaviors.[2]

This manager was at a precontemplation stage—the stage at which there is no intention to change behavior in the foreseeable future. This manager couldn't acknowledge that there were actual problems and issues that needed to be changed. She needed to get to the contemplation stage, where she could start to understand that she, in fact, had issues and problems that needed attention and work.

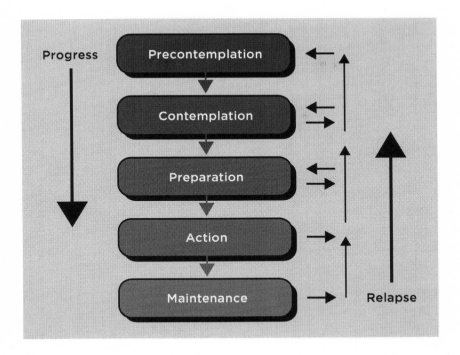

The process of changing usually involves a substantial commitment of time, effort, and emotion and the self awareness to identify that change is required to grow. When I realized this person was a problem and that I would never effectively change their behaviors, it was too late; the damage had been done. The slow rot had infected many of our other people. From this lesson, I have come to understand that problems can often be subtle and slow burning, and not always glaringly obvious.

CEO coach Cameron Herold says, "You need to work at bringing the right people in, and you need to work at getting the wrong people out."

Cameron Herold also says, "The cost of keeping the wrong person can be up to 15 times his or her annual salary. As an example, if you had an employee earning $100,000 a year and you know he's the wrong person, it actually may be costing the company $1.5 million a year to keep him."[3]

Go with Your Gut

I knew deep in my gut something was off, but I did not take the time to really investigate that feeling. Oftentimes, we are sent messages from our gut, and we choose not to listen closely enough. Gut instinct is also known as "the first brain." The gray matter in your brain receives messages from your gut—instincts and observations you should be mindful of. I shouldn't have disregarded these feelings, as my gut was one of my best navigational devices when I was young, and it still is today. My gut generally tells me when I am steering in the wrong direction or potentially making a bad decision.

My gut instinct had a lot to say about letting this manager and team remain in place. The worst decision is to ignore what you are feeling. Being proactive, rather than reactive, allows you to do things on your own timeline. Take the time to truly examine what you are feeling, conduct an Alphabet Exercise—assigning a grade from A (best fit) to D (worst fit)— consider reaching out to managers in your firm to seek additional guidance, and plan to make a change *on your terms*.

Creating and enforcing your MVPs (mission, values, purpose) will help you keep the right people in your firm. It will guide your hiring and help you build a team of competent leaders. But don't stop your involvement after you hire the right people. Provide a road map, offer training and development, give guidance, and allow them to offer ideas, suggestions, and recommendations so that they may grow into happy, competent employees.

⌂ PUNCH LIST

- **Strive for excellence.** No matter what job you're hired to do, consider opportunities to upsell and expand your customer base, even if your colleagues are content with doing as little as possible.

- **Manage processes from start to finish.** Keep your focus on the customer, but don't neglect in-house support. Be attentive to all levels and aspects of the fulfillment teams.

- **Remediate rot.** The wrong person in a position, or a wrong attitude, spreads quickly and infects other people in the company.

- **Pinpoint the issue.** Remove the offender instead of replacing those around him or her. The latter runs up the costs and does nothing to preserve the culture and quality of your business.

- **Understand change.** Know what is changeable. There are five stages one must undergo to get to lasting change: precontemplation, contemplation, preparation, action, and maintenance.

- **Listen to your gut.** Gut instinct is also known as "the first brain."

Reset—Reposition—Rebuild

"You may not control all the events that happen to you,
but you can decide not to be reduced by them."

—MAYA ANGELOU

Before you start any renovation or build, you create a budget. Say you are renovating your kitchen, gutting the existing one, and creating a brand-new one. The overall price to do that might be $150,000, but there will be allocations created for each portion of the project (e.g., $35,000 for appliances, $55,000 for cabinetry, etc.). To be safe, you should always create a 10 percent differential or buffer in case something unanticipated comes up that is not covered in the budget. Every now and then, you will uncover something that is so damaging to the budget it becomes a 30–40 percent increase on the entire scope of the project. This is a blindside, something completely unexpected that is very upsetting!

On November 11, 2017, I was fired from my own company—a company I founded and ran successfully for thirty-one and a half years. To say the experience was surreal would be an understatement. It was cold, unceremonious, and totally unexpected. The new owner terminated me through a text and email message. I was never allowed back into my own company and building.

Ten other loyal colleagues were terminated the next day—all together in one room with two armed police officers supervising. Two of those fired were six-figure executives—second- and third-in-command at my firm, employed by me for over twenty-two years. They were never allowed back to their desks, nor were they allowed to say goodbye to their fellow colleagues, people they had worked alongside for decades. I spent a huge chunk of my life working with those people and in that building. It was devastating.

While the group firing took place, a few of the employees' immediate personal possessions were haphazardly tossed on the floor in a fire exit hallway for them to hurriedly grab on their way out. The employees were later allowed to pick up their hastily packed personal items outside in the front parking lot. If ever there was a road map on "what not to do," this was it!

Do It with Dignity

When I reflect on that time, I see all the missed opportunities to lead with dignity and grace. We have a responsibility as leaders to handle these extremely difficult moments with compassion and empathy. People adapt faster to the heartbreak of a loved one's death than they do to being unemployed.[1] As leaders, even in our darkest hour and most uncomfortable moments, we can take a chance, be vulnerable, and open ourselves up to the possibility that our employees might be willing to share the burden of supporting the company.

In 2020, Gravity Payments, a credit card payment processing firm, was losing $1.5 million a month. They had three months until they would go out of business. They were faced with few choices: either eliminate a great team that would be difficult to rebuild, or absorb massive financial losses and potentially lose the firm. But CEO and founder Dan Price said there was another way, and he proved it. The solution was to act as a team. "Your team is so much smarter than you. Give power to your people, be honest and democratic. They will find solutions that you can't see." Instead of making any layoffs, Price asked his employees to anonymously volunteer for pay cuts.[2]

His team volunteered nearly half a million dollars a month from their salaries, while some even offered their total pay. "Businesses love to talk about caring for their people, but the conventional wisdom is, what really matters in these situations is your balance sheet," says Dan Price.[3] There will come times in your firm when you are forced to make extraordinarily difficult decisions, ones that will be gut-wrenching. But just because you must do something difficult doesn't mean you have to execute it in poor fashion or without remaining aligned to your core values and mission.

As my business entered its thirtieth year, just a year and a half before my unpleasant departure, I started to contemplate my firm's future. Hitting the back nine of my career caused me to reflect. I had at least another decade to go in business and had anticipated a well-executed and tightly planned transition period with time to look back on all our accomplishments and years of service. This decision to sell my company took me two years to make, as I was deeply concerned about my legacy and the future of my trusted and loyal employees.

When considering the sale of my business, I had a trusted advisor bring several prospects to my door for potential acquisition. The firm I chose promised a bright future to my employees, and their MVPs—mission, values, purpose—seemed completely aligned with our own. They assured me they would not dismantle our team or change our business; they wanted us to continue operating autonomously. The owner seemed smitten with our brand and spoke of transparency in almost every meeting we had.

Because I grew up amid so many uncertainties, it was very important to me that I uncover and mitigate as many potential problems as possible and choose the right buyer for my firm. This was my baby, and I wanted someone to love it as I did—to nurture and grow it. My employees deserved greater opportunities for advancement, and I was convinced this new company would give it to them.

A Proper Transition

As much as you dream about starting a company, there will come a time when you must start planning your exit strategy. When it was time for me to transition out of the firm, I envisioned a retirement party with me giving a poignant speech thanking everyone who had stayed with me loyally all those years. I planned on sitting around with my colleagues and recounting war stories and staffing foibles, laughing as we reminisced about our famed candidates and customers by name.

I fully expected setting up meetings with customers to express my deepest gratitude for their loyalty and business; some of these relationships spanned twenty-five years. I wanted to thank them sincerely for the many years they'd allowed us to serve their needs and share in their lives. And most importantly, I thought I would share a nostalgic goodbye with my loyal employees who remained to continue the great work we had started thirty-one years ago.

Manage Your Message

Clear communication and conveying a distinct message are critical during a transition from one long partnership to a new one. I wanted to ensure my employees and customers were left in good hands. Ideally, letters and social announcements would have been sent with a plan of action for diligent and timely verbal follow-up. I would have personally met with many of our loyal consultants whom we deployed daily in the field, some of whom I had represented for thirty years. Many had started with me as high school graduates or freshmen in college; I'd seen them through their first job after graduation and up through the ranks of management, and many years later, I'd placed their children.

Without our loyal and trusted deployable talent, many customer relationships might not have been forged, built, and sustained successfully for so many decades.

When you strive to be a company with a strong culture, you can't be absentminded when it comes to the small details, even in a crisis situation. It is paramount to critique every important message carefully before delivering it to your employees and customers. If the message has emotion around it, consider an additional set of eyes from a trusted advisor to ensure the proper message is received. As a

> *When a transition occurs, it is vital to send a branded message to your customers, assuring them that service will remain consistent and high-quality.*

leader, you walk a fine line with communication. A message could be well-intended but perceived by your audience as completely off-putting, insensitive, or lacking the emotion they expect.

When I had to respond to a negative customer review, I had a policy of writing my rebuttal and then saving it in my draft file overnight. This afforded me time for clarity and to ensure the message had the proper tone and spirit.

How you treat, communicate with, and speak to people is an essential part of building and nurturing relationships. People rely on a consistent message, and as a leader, you must provide that consistency to them.

Control What You Can

For thirty-one years, I worked in my own firm, and then, suddenly, I did not. I didn't get the chance to walk around and store away my final memories. I did not get to say goodbye—not to the place and not to the people. These were people I'd worked with and shared my life with for decades, most of whom were dear friends and many of whom I considered to be family and my support system. This affected me deeply. Since I lacked a strong family foundation, I had spent the time creating one at my company, coming to rely on and love these people as if they were my very own family. Because they were.

I had worked for over thirty years building a company and filling it with people I treasured—and now they were gone.

The greatest fear that I have always faced, the lever that drives me every day, is *the fear of losing everything I have*. Naturally, this comes from my upbringing and watching my father lose everything we had. So when this unexpected firing happened, it triggered that fear. Although I was comfortable financially, given the compensation I received, I was unsteady emotionally due to losing the relationships I'd forged over many years with my colleagues. And although I was disappointed with the outcome, this situation was not mine to control.

You must recognize that as a leader, you cannot control everything. You can set things up so processes go smoothly, but in the end, you can't control the outcomes.

I've dealt with adversity all my life, gutting my way through each bad problem I encountered. Countless Saturdays were spent on the stoop waiting for a mother who never arrived. Promises were broken, and time and time again, I was faced with raging disappointment from the absent parenting I received from my mother and father. I fought my entire life to make something of myself, to be different and better than my family, and to push the boundaries of what I wanted to accomplish for myself.

I vowed that I would never live a life like they did, I would always value and cherish what I earned, and I would hold on to what I had and not foolishly lose it to debt and irresponsibility. You see, I have dealt with adversity since I was born, and this—this was merely another temporary setback.

Overcoming Adversity

So how do you overcome challenging situations? Try these actions.

- **Focus on facts.** Don't let irrational thoughts cloud your perspective.

- **Soar with eagles.** Surround yourself with uplifting, strong-willed individuals who will guide, support, and direct you.

- **Work on self-resiliency.** Spend time working on your mental and physical stamina.

- **Seek balance.** Strive for a lifestyle balance and an internal balance, utilizing both your logical and emotional brains.

- **Maintain a consistent schedule.** Hold yourself accountable and keep looking forward.

I always like to remember a quote by Carl Jung: "I am not what happened to me, I am what I choose to become."

⌂ PUNCH LIST

- **Do it with dignity.** Treat others the way you'd want to be treated. And remember, your word is your reputation.

- **Look to your people.** Before considering drastic measures, have faith that your people believe in your brand and care for your company as much as you do.

- **Keep the end in mind.** As much as you dream about starting a company, there will come a time when you must start planning your exit strategy.

- **Manage your message.** When a transition occurs, it's important to send a branded message to your customers, assuring them that services will remain consistent and high-quality.

- **Follow the forty-eight-hour rule.** Never respond to an emotional message immediately. When responding to a negative customer review, for example, don't shoot off a quick rejoinder. Take some time and maybe ask someone else to look it over.

- **Do what you say.** How we treat, communicate with, and speak to people is an essential part of building and nurturing relationships.

- **Control what you can.** We can't control everything. You can set things up so processes go smoothly, but in the end, you can't control the outcomes.

PART 6

Cleanup

C leanup is the dirty work no one wants to do, but it provides you with a clean slate to work with. It removes all the bad old debris and offers you a blank space filled with endless possibilities. Cleanup in the remodeling industry reminds me so much of what one needs to do with their business and its people.

Oftentimes, we refuse to do the cleanup we know we need to do. Instead, we hold on to people because we are emotionally invested in them, ultimately doing a disservice not only to ourselves but also to them. It is important to release employees who aren't the right fit, and bring in people who will move your businesses forward. The right management team will hold you accountable and help ensure that you have the right people in the right seats. Maintain a consistent pipeline of talent, and you will not be held hostage by the wrong people. That would be dire for the growth of your firm.

Train Up Your Leaders

"The happiest people I know are always evaluating and improving themselves. The unhappy people are usually evaluating and judging others."

—LISA VILLA PROSEN

Our most recent renovation project was a small Cape Cod on a spectacular piece of property that had suffered years of landscape neglect; it was severely overgrown with downed dead trees and poison ivy. The house itself was something right out of the seventies, with lots of bright floral wallpaper, low ceilings, small rooms, and pedestal sinks. One of the bathrooms was so small that your knees touched the wall when you sat on the toilet! Out of all the projects my husband and I have tackled, this one was the most complex and by far the hardest. Yet this property is now the most beloved.

The house was U-shaped, with a large courtyard in the middle of the property. Everyone who saw the house prior to the renovation advised us to remove the courtyard and turn it into actual square footage. I was the visionary who saw a glimpse of Italy: a pergola with dangling grapevines or Bougainvillea shading us from the midday sun. I envisioned a spectacular farmhouse table holding eighteen to twenty of my dearest friends and family. I eventually won the battle, turning that vision into a reality. My husband would agree that the courtyard is now a spectacular focal point and the very heart of our outdoor living plan.

Renovating involves a tremendous amount of planning. There is a structured plan that must be followed rigorously in order for the many subcontractors to do their work at exactly the right time. The general contractor carefully directs this process and instructs each subcontractor when to arrive and what they should be doing. As a leader, you must devote time and attention to training and developing your employees so that they too are able to work independently.

Training and Development

When it comes to leadership, development and training are vital to the long-term success of your employees. So why, in most cases,

By incrementally increasing job responsibilities each year, as well as providing training and development, we were able to extend our junior-level employees' tenure by one-and-a-half to three years.

are employees provided zero training after being promoted to a new role? This is a big mistake and will set the employee up for failure.

First, without leadership training or coaching, the employee won't expand their knowledge. They may also have difficulty gaining respect from their former peers, now direct reports. Employees who are promoted into their first management role might be quite sheep-ish about their new responsibilities, or even quite bullish; neither trait is desirable when starting a new management journey.

Resourceful vs. Sheepish

I had two commonly noticeable personality types in my newly promoted leaders. There were those who were very independent, resourceful, and happy to hone their new management skill set on their own. The other personality type needed an extreme amount of guidance and handholding. They were not proactive and didn't voluntarily seek out resources to support their new management position.

You can't expect your newly appointed leaders to go out and find their own training, and you shouldn't want them to because it might not meet the expectations of your business. If you don't cre-ate a training process prior to promoting your staff, your people will behave according to what they believe is best for the company. Additionally, when you leave someone to their own devices, you run the risk of them developing bad habits that will then need to be corrected. You could potentially have to go back and untrain these bad habits before they are fully formed.

A Developed Process

Here is a process you can consider:

1. Ensure that your management team sees the value of adopting management training for newly appointed man-agers. They must do their part to mentor and develop your new leaders. It will be detrimental if you can't get management aligned with this process.

2. Create a detailed outline of expectations for training, including key managers and time blocks. Schedule time with your trainee at the end of each week to review the training and ensure everyone is following the process.

3. Assign your employee to various mentors based on each mentor's key attributes. For example, if one manager has incredible time-management skills, have them provide that portion of training. If another manager has achieved great success in sales and customer development, assign that person to showcase those key attributes.

4. Have your trainee read a business book that you believe closely aligns with your MVPs. Give them a deadline, and ask them for key takeaways, including what areas are applicable to your business. Compare their takeaways to yours, and see if their comments line up with your vision for the business. This exercise will give you a glimpse into their mind and how they interpret customer service, value, and expectations. If you determine their takeaways aren't what you had hoped, a small flag will go up in the back of your mind. Be mindful of this as training continues; your gut will tell you more.

5. Consider making use of outside resources—such as an industry expert, a coach, or a series of webinars or seminars—to complement your internal training. Bringing in an industry expert will validate your training and provide an accredited point of view to your employees. Outside coaches and experts bring new energy, excitement, and renewed belief to what you are saying every day. This person should echo all your daily mantras.

Assess, Understand, Train

When hiring someone externally for your management team, the same process is required, even though they might already have developed most of these skill sets. Consider using skills assessments to gauge strengths and weaknesses and pinpoint areas that might need further development.

Below are examples of assessments you can use to identify your employees' strengths and areas that need improvement.

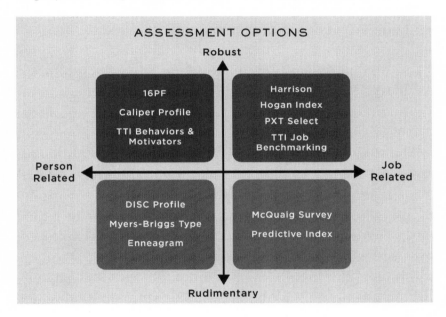

The top-left quadrant of this diagram shows us the robust personal assessments, which provide an in-depth analysis of a person's behaviors and characteristics.

The top-right quadrant of this diagram shows us the robust job-related assessments, which provide an in-depth analysis of a person's job-related preferred tasks and behaviors.

The bottom-left quadrant of this diagram shows us the

rudimentary personal assessments, which provide an overview of a person's behaviors and characteristics.

The bottom-right quadrant of this diagram shows us the rudimentary job-related assessments, which provide an overview of a person's job-related preferred tasks and behaviors.[1]

Like a good general contractor, you must lay out a concise process to teach your management trainees the behaviors and skills you want in your firm, as well as get them aligned with your values. Values can't be aspirational—they must guide how you run the business and be infused in the training your firm provides.

Broken-Nose Commitment

One of my dear friends has a value at his company that he calls the "Broken-Nose Commitment." This value comes with a story that he gets to share over and over again—to each and every potential hire—as a way to showcase his company's firmly rooted values. It goes like this.

One of the warehouse managers was working in their plant when he broke his nose right on the warehouse floor. Blood went everywhere, and it was clear he had done some serious damage to his face. He immediately went to the emergency room, only to return to work a few hours later. Everybody was shocked and amazed to see him back at work. That is how "Broken-Nose Commitment" became one of their values. This manager cared deeply about the firm and put its customers above all else.

When training new managers, share stories like these to help them understand the heart and soul of your company. Your values must come from you, be genuine and meaningful, and be used as a management tool for your people.

⌂ PUNCH LIST

- **Develop your leaders.** Give them training even before you promote them into leadership positions. This is vital to the long-term success of your employees.

- **Identify leaders' personas.** Some people jump into new leadership roles with self-starting zeal, while others need more guidance. Be ready to work with both types.

- **Remember that one size doesn't suit all.** There are many ways to help cultivate leadership qualities among new leaders. Be willing to adapt.

- **Showcase your "Broken-Nose Commitments."** Use stories to help your new employees understand your company culture.

Commit to Care and Consistency

"You've got to be rigorous in your appraisal system.
The biggest cowards are managers who don't let their
people know where they stand."

—JACK WELCH

Through thirty-five years of experience as an entrepreneur and avid remodeler, I've had plenty of encounters with poor performance and problematic scenarios. What I have found to be the best remedy is straightforward communications, a three-strike documentation system, and diligent action.

I only had to fire one contractor and one architect in all my years in the remodeling industry, and both terminations were a pleasure. This particular architect came highly recommended and was extremely well known in his field; however, he wasn't interested in listening to his customers' ideas. He was only concerned with building elaborate structures, despite the fact we—his customers—wanted something more practical and functional. Clearly, our ideas were not aligned.

No matter how much my husband and I tried to explain what we wanted, that architect insisted on using only his designs and would become very defensive. He was rude and dismissive, and our only course of action was to terminate him from our project. We ended up finding another local architect who was amazing—extremely flexible and open to our ideas and input. He has remained our architect through two other projects and has become a very good friend.

Of course, it is much easier to terminate someone for cause or someone who is terrible. However, all terminations involve a delicate process that needs to be carefully managed and documented.

Terminating people is inevitable, uncomfortable, and upsetting. But it can be done with professionalism, grace, and dignity—and should be done this way consistently throughout the course of your business. Don't expect your employees to always understand why you are terminating someone, especially if that person is affable and a good cultural fit. What your staff *will* appreciate is the expected process of consistency.

Speaking from Experience

When I was sixteen, I got fired. I will never forget it. I needed extra money, so I took an evening job as a waitress at a lovely restaurant in Norwalk. They made me set a table, open a bottle of wine, and answer a series of questions pertaining to "serving the customers." I figured I'd be a shoo-in for this job, as my values regarding customer service clearly aligned with theirs.

My first night happened to be a lovely Saturday evening. It was cool out, and I was assigned the patio, the room farthest from the kitchen. In order to get from the kitchen to the patio, I had to go through a set of double doors, up a flight of stairs, through the main dining room, and through another set of double doors. I had a table for eight, and lobsters were the special that night. My table ordered eight lobster dinners. Once I loaded up my tray with the eight lobsters, I started carrying the tray on my hip, as I couldn't tolerate the weight load if I carried it over my head. The manager, who happened to be in the kitchen, immediately saw what I was doing and yelled at me to carry over my head only. I tried to explain that I was not able to do so, but he angrily waved me away.

Balancing the heavy tray in the air, I made it through the first set of double doors successfully and got up to the top of the stairs. I took a momentary break before making my way through the packed dining room to the second set of double doors. As I started to go through, someone came in from the other side and clipped the corner of my tray.

I lost control of the entire tray, and eight lobster dinners went cascading across the patio floor. It was one of the most embarrassing moments of my life! When I returned to the kitchen, the manager fired me in front of everyone. He didn't take a moment to bring me into a private room and hear my side of the story. He made an immediate assumption and humiliated me in front of a crowd—after I had already humiliated myself!

Off-Boarding Consistency

It is important to off-board people with as much professionalism and dignity as you onboarded them with. These actions will leave a lasting impression on them. You don't want to fail in the off-boarding process and potentially create a negative experience. This could damage your hiring reputation and culture long term.

Don't allow a negative detractor to go out into the world armed with ammunition against your company; this could ruin the "brag behind the brand" reputation you worked so hard to build. A consumer is 21 percent more likely to share a negative experience than a positive one.[1]

Let's first look at the appraisal process. I highly recommend that you have a strong appraisal process to measure, manage, and document your employees' performance. Employees should be told candidly how they are performing. Ask yourself this: "How can someone improve if they aren't informed, comfortably critiqued, and coached?"

Appraisal Apprehension

The review process should be done annually, semi-annually, or quarterly. Insist that the process you create is followed consistently. Our most successful review process was this one: We kept the questions very short and aligned them with our values. We used multiple-choice questions and included open text boxes for notes and comments. And finally, we created a very simple electronic version of our reviewing process to ensure it got done in a timely manner.

Prior to this process, we had a manual review with open text boxes, but people felt this was overwhelming and took too long. Multiple choice is simpler and removes some of the emotion that goes into reviewing people candidly.

Also consider a two-way reviewing method. This method allows employees to weigh in on your performance as a leader and make recommendations. At our firm, we had a two-way review process both asking for our employees' opinions and providing feedback on their performance based on our values. During our review periods, we would have a directors meeting where we performed an Alphabet Exercise (A to D) on all our employees to ensure our management team was in full alignment.

This exercise consisted of two extremely important areas for us: culture and performance. The left side of the sheet had cultural attributes (our MVPs); the bottom of the sheet had the employees' sales quotas and KPIs. We then used our A, B, C, and D grading system. If the employee received below a C, they were moved to the "consider termination" column.

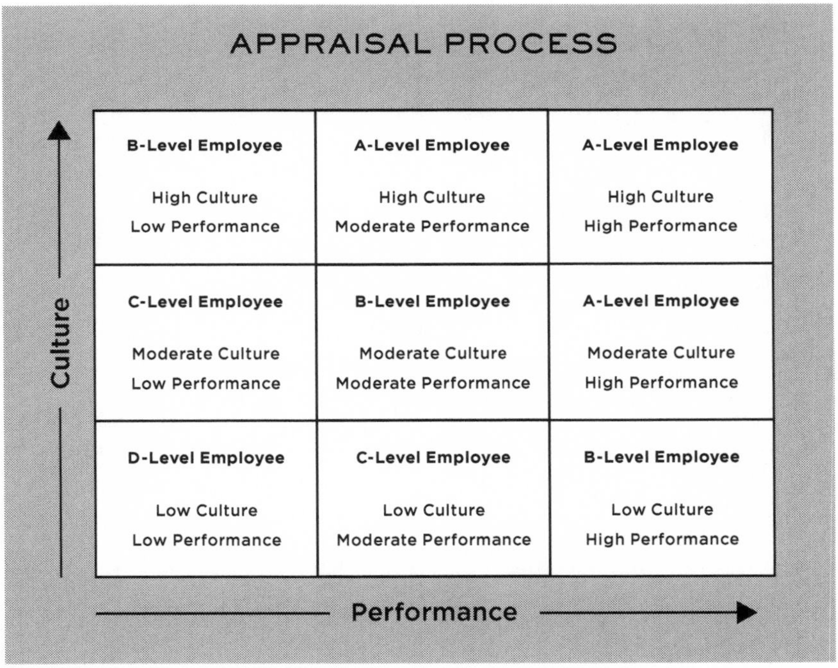
APPRAISAL PROCESS
B-Level Employee
High Culture
Low Performance
A-Level Employee
High Culture
Moderate Performance
A-Level Employee
High Culture
High Performance
C-Level Employee
Moderate Culture
Low Performance
B-Level Employee
Moderate Culture
Moderate Performance
A-Level Employee
Moderate Culture
High Performance
D-Level Employee
Low Culture
Low Performance
C-Level Employee
Low Culture
Moderate Performance
B-Level Employee
Low Culture
High Performance
Culture
Performance

This exercise was done with our entire management team present, each weighing in on our employees. The managers would add the employees' names to sticky notes and place them on the white board grid. They then had to give their reasoning behind their grade and placement.

After we reviewed our entire organization with our management team, my partner and I would do the same exercise *on* our management team. This removed all the emotion from the reviewing and firing process. When we determined someone was not performing to their expected sales level or had other performance issues, we made a list of areas that needed immediate improvement. If the employee was off on their sales quota, we documented the discrepancy and determined what performance numbers they would need to get back on track.

We then had a face-to-face meeting with the employee to discuss the items of concern, prepared a written statement of our discussions, and had a copy signed by the employee and placed in their employee folder in human resources.

Three-Strike System

We also created an action plan with a timeframe—either thirty, sixty, or ninety days—during which the employee was expected to change their performance behaviors. If their performance remained the same at our second performance meeting, they were given a second warning and told what the outcome would be if they didn't immediately improve. If, by the third meeting, they still showed no improvement, the employee was terminated.

If declining job performance is the issue, no one should be blindsided. Give the employee a chance to repair it.

Apart from terminations for cause, meaning a worker did something wrong—stealing, lying, sexual harassment, and so on—most of our terminations were done face-to-face with dignity and professionalism. Jack Welch once said, "No person should be surprised when being terminated from their job due to performance."

Every person has challenges of one kind or another. It is important to study those challenges and evaluate how to overcome them. You may remember that Lee Iacocca was fired from Ford Motor Corporation—only to later rebuild Chrysler when it was losing millions of dollars due to recalls.[2] By adhering to a three-strike process, you are giving your employees the chance to improve and show you their strengths.

Laying off people is far worse, as an employer, than firing someone for cause. But if your firm is in peril, it must be done to preserve the business and all the remaining employees. As a leader, your obligation is to the organization, not to an individual person. There could come a time when you are in this situation; perhaps you overextended your company, lost a large customer, or got hit by a recession or pandemic. People won't necessarily remember the circumstances of their termination, but they will remember how they were treated from the very beginning to the very end of their employment at your company.

Laying off good workers because of a recession or other extenuating circumstance is much more upsetting than having to terminate someone for poor performance. It's also terrible for them because they aren't at fault in any way. But the mere act of someone leaving your firm, whether because of their job performance or your company performance, is stressful and upsetting.

The Importance of Timing

Recently, Ford announced that it would lay off approximately seven thousand people in its workforce. CEO Jim Hackett said this layoff is different: "We have moved away from past practices in some regions where team members who were separated had to leave immediately with their belongings, instead giving people the choice to stay for a few days to wrap up and say goodbye."[3]

Whether you choose to keep your employees on or have them leave immediately—each situation has its own set of repercussions. Most managers have the ability to judge whether an employee can stay and maintain their composure. But the bottom line is this: Most people who are terminated will be upset, regardless of the circumstances, and people need time to process and grieve. They will go through a series of different emotions.

In a few instances, employees will react with desperation and potentially do some very bad things, even illegal things. You might think that granting your employees the time to say their goodbyes is a good and kind thing; however, it may put a large burden and guilt on those employees who remain at the firm, leaving them feeling awkward and ill at ease.

It may be easier to have the departing employees leave right away; then you can speak to them outside of work after they have had time to process, grieve, and collect themselves. Personally, I have seen departing employees create a lot of unneeded negative drama that stays with the remaining staff long after they depart.

According to CEO coach Cameron Herold, companies tend to wait four to six months on average from the point that management knows they should cut the cord to the time they let that individual go. There's a point when you know that it's not working, and you either need to have that direct conversation or make the cut. But many people often second-guess it and wait too long.[4]

Be Part of the Process

No matter what you do, no single process will be seamless. The most important part of these scenarios is that you, the owner, "show up" and provide a humane and dignified process. Be courageous and mindful about treating people as you would expect to be treated; follow a consistent, well-thought-out process; and execute that process flawlessly. The times that I did not personally terminate someone or speak to them during their departure, I was left with an overwhelming amount of guilt and dissatisfaction—especially knowing that most people joined our firm because of me.

Be courageous. Do what is right, and show your employees that you carefully considered this decision. When you operate a firm, these situations are inevitable; having an established process and properly executing that process are critical to your firm's culture and future reputation.

Remember, before you even get to the termination stage, be sure you've talked directly with the employee about performance. Oftentimes, managers are too afraid to confront their employees about shortcomings. This is unacceptable, and you could potentially end up terminating a perfectly capable employee who just needed a small course correction.

Deliberate Deliveries

One of our top performers was extremely sensitive to any form of critiquing, making it almost impossible to confront her without really upsetting her. This prevented a lot of people from approaching her when it was most needed. Knowing that my advice would only further her success and our firm's success, I got into the habit of asking her for permission to give her constructive advice.

This allowed her the opportunity to put herself in the mindset to receive feedback.

She soon realized that we weren't trying to upset her but to build up her skills. This process made giving her feedback more comfortable for us all, and it created a trusting, safe environment for her.

Young people are particularly receptive to this form of critiquing because it redirects the focus onto their work and feels less like an attack on them personally.

Just Ask

Another way to understand how to work with people is to simply ask. Take the time to ask everyone that you manage how they like to receive feedback. This creates a very comfortable rapport and helps establish strong, trusting relationships.

Throughout our thirty-plus years, we rarely terminated someone who genuinely tried to do the job at hand. Most people want to succeed and perform well. Rather, a termination is often the result of a misaligned hire or poor fit. Therefore, it is critical to work on your talent acquisition strategy daily and ensure you have a strong hiring team and process in place, ready to hire the right people into the right seats.

⌂ PUNCH LIST

- -

- **Welcome employee feedback.** Consider a two-way review process that allows employees to provide feedback and share their opinions about the company.

- **Mitigate negative detractors.** If you must terminate someone, regardless of the reason, be certain that their off-boarding experience is managed with a high degree of care.

- **Eat the frog.** Be equipped to make hard decisions swiftly. Don't procrastinate and delay the inevitable; be present and show up when these difficult issues arise.

- **Tailor your delivery.** If one of your employees is sensitive to critiquing, consider different methods of offering feedback (e.g., asking for their permission to do so).

Break Down and Break Through

"Change doesn't occur when you are comfortable,
but when you're being tested in some way."

—JEFFREY KOTTLER

Before you buy a house, you almost always conduct a home inspection. You want to perform due diligence on such a large purchase and find out what is underneath all the timber and sheetrock. Unfortunately, building inspectors today generally perform a surface inspection, quite often missing a lot of the more problematic issues. In their defense, a lot of the areas that should be inspected are difficult to get to, either buried in walls or covered by plaster or sheetrock. Therefore, every now and then, you buy a real lemon.

For me, the transition into no longer being the owner of my firm was not easy. It's a radical change to go from being part of something so important—something you dedicated your life to—to suddenly *not* being part of it. Like most leaders and entrepreneurs, I was defined by my work. But then it was gone—without any warning, without giving me a chance to prepare.

Leaving behind my cherished colleagues was overwhelming. It left me with a tremendous amount of guilt and uncertainty. These were people I spent years protecting, making sure that their positions were never threatened by a downturn or recession. These were the people I'd stuck with through thick and thin, and they'd shielded me. Yet suddenly, there was nothing tethering us together. Exactly what I had worked so hard to avoid ended up happening anyway!

Transitional Moments

After spending thirty-one years at a company, the very next day I no longer had a place to report to, my entire routine changed, and I had a bunch of pieces that didn't seem to fit anywhere anymore. This reaffirmed for me that treating people with dignity and respect is vital, especially when making difficult decisions. It made me truly understand what it is like to be terminated and how important the messaging of such an intimate event is.

No one really remembers how something begins—but they surely always remember how something ends.

You see, in my opinion, true leaders must set the example for their employees by showing them that even during difficult times, when making hard decisions, all people must be treated with dignity and respect throughout the entire process.

As a leader, you must prepare for all the uncertainties that come along with the job. You will face countless surprise decisions that you have to respond to quickly. I remember the recession of 2008–2009, when our financial divisions fell off a cliff. We were chugging along nicely, averaging about $6 million in our combined financial services and accounting and finance divisions, and—*bam*—within weeks, the business had deteriorated to below a million dollars.

Diagnose, Decide, Deliver

These situations come up quite often when you are a leader, and there is little time to prepare. During the recession, I gathered the two team leads. We discussed our options, carefully pored over the finances, and then communicated our plan to each team. We were fortunate enough to have some very seasoned people whom we could deploy to other divisions. We removed four of the weaker performers, sitting down with them and having honest conversations. We continued to meet weekly with each team and committed to focused, extensive customer outreach to discuss any potential ways we could be of service to our customers. We ultimately came out of this downturn and rebuilt those departments into very high-performing divisions.

I distinctly remember 9/11 and the absolute horror of that day. We were in our Stamford location at the time, all huddled up in our break room watching the horror unfold.

A dear customer's brother lost his life that day in one of the Twin Tower buildings in New York City; each one of us was affected in some way. For the first three to five days, we allowed our staff to grieve and express themselves however they felt most comfortable. I kept my doors open every day to speak to anyone who needed support and guidance, as did the leaders in our human resources department and other executives. We offered grief counseling for anyone in need and strongly encouraged our staff to seek comfort and solace in any way they wanted. I remember almost every vivid detail of that day at work and will likely never forget. When you are a leader, your people will often turn to you in times of crisis to see how you conduct yourself, and quite often, their response will mirror yours.

Eventually, there comes a time when you must address the more difficult and uncomfortable issues. After five days, the time came to get back to work. It was extremely important to explain to our staff that our customers needed to hear from us. By getting back to a routine, we were providing normalcy in a time when nothing was normal. By talking to our customers, we showed them that we cared and could comfort and help them.

Being a leader during a time of adversity can be extremely challenging. Stuart Cross, founder of Morgan Cross Consulting and author of *CEO Strategy Handbook*, reviews what a leader can focus on during times of adversity.

5 CS OF LEADING IN TIMES OF ADVERSITY

1. **Credibility:** Competency and credibility are the bedrock of leadership.

2. **Clarity:** Ambiguity is the enemy of leadership.

3. **Consistency:** Communication and requests should be clear and consistent.

4. **Confidence:** A leader should be confident, a strong presence, and available.

5. **Communication:** Important messages should be repeatedly pushed out to team members.[1]

Recover and Rebound

Many times throughout the course of owning your own business, you will have such traumatic events thrust on you that you will feel you won't likely recover. I have come to realize the loss of my work family and the fate of most of the great people at my firm upset me in a way I will most likely never fully recover from.

However, I have been tested my whole life, constantly overcoming obstacles and hurdles far greater than this. The pain of having such a dysfunctional family will remain with me over the entire course of my life, and the family that I often dream of will never be. But I am truly blessed to have made a beautiful life for myself with my husband, daughter, and soon-to-be son-in-law and have the luxury of enjoying their large and beautiful family.

These tests are what make us stronger and open us up to truly being able to see what is important and what is next.

I was finished with my business, and it was time to move on. I chose a firm I thought would bring new and exciting career opportunities and growth for my remaining loyal and dedicated staff. It certainly did not turn out the way I envisioned it, and that has to be okay.

There are certain things you simply cannot control, and you cannot get caught up in "What happened to me?" and become a victim. You must take the cards you are dealt and play them to the very best of your ability. Indecision is the thief of opportunity. When you change your perspective, you create opportunities.

Starting with the end helped me focus on the beginning again; I'd used the art of serving and engaging as the basis for a very strong platform to start my first business—and now I would use it to start my second one.

⌂ PUNCH LIST

- **Lead with courage.** Things won't always go your way, but keep moving forward. You'll get there, and you'll take your people with you.

- **Have empathy.** Be patient and empathetic, especially in stressful times. Allow people to grieve if needed, but then get back to your routine.

- **Apply the 5 Cs.** When times are hard, use credibility, clarity, consistency, confidence, and communication.

- **Be bold.** Indecision is the thief of opportunity.

- **Make a move.** If your first few attempts at starting something don't work out, keep moving forward, and other opportunities will present themselves.

Refute "Counter-feit" Offers

"Job counteroffers are ways companies avoid the
annoyances of losing employees at the wrong time."

—JAY WREN[1]

I have always been particularly empathetic to the building
industry when it comes to staffing crew members. It seems
builders are either understaffed or overstaffed but never staffed
perfectly to suit their current building needs. In slowdowns, I have
seen contractors cut almost their entire crew, and then I've seen
them scrambling to bring those same crew members back on their
payroll when business picks up.

Worse than that, I have seen crew members walk off an existing
job, leaving the general contractor in a dire situation. When an

employee leaves abruptly, the company is faced with an uncomfortable and frustrating situation, as the customer obligations still need to be fulfilled. Nothing is worse than an unpredictable resignation with no replacements on the horizon.

Counteroffer Perils

Sometimes cleaning up after a situation is out of your control, as in the case of resignations. Resignations are going to happen, and they will inevitably come at the worst possible time when you feel you can least tolerate it. Because of these unscheduled events, you must invest consistent time and effort into building your talent pipeline in preparation for these exact moments. In the absence of a good talent pipeline, your back will be up against the wall, forcing you to make decisions that could prove to be the wrong ones.

In our firm, we coached our customers against making counteroffers, by which I mean offering an employee more money if they agree to stay in their job. We were staffing executives—professionals—who were counseling our customers daily against the perils of extending a counteroffer to an employee who had just resigned.

As part of our recruitment process, we also openly advised job-seeking employees not to accept a counteroffer from their current employer, as this action is a short-term solution and often masks the real reasons an employee is leaving their current position. When potential job seekers did receive a counteroffer, we asked them a set of defining questions, like the ones that follow, which helped draw out the real reason they were leaving a position.

1. What is the primary reason you decided to look for another job?

2. Are you leaving your current position because of
    money? If not, why?

3. How is this counteroffer (from your current employer)
    going to change your reasons for leaving?

Counteroffers rarely work out favorably for either party. The employee remembers only a few months later the real reasons they were disenchanted with the position, and the employer has an employee who has mentally checked out and no longer believes in the company's mission. Statistics show that if you accept a counteroffer, the probability of voluntarily leaving in six months or being let go within one year is extremely high. National statistics indicate that 89 percent of people who accept counteroffers are gone in six months.[2]

Money's Not Everything

Let us think about this for a minute. If an employee is motivated enough to go through the application and interview process for another job opportunity, they are done with their career at your firm. When people resign, they are done with their current job for multiple reasons, and they're ready to move on. They will be only "temporarily" satisfied with a counteroffer. The excitement of a few more bucks wears off after a few months, and they are right back to where they started. Their reasons for considering a switch in employers do not go away. Their actions sour their colleagues' opinions of them and the company, and trust has been broken.

Money is not the sole problem. In fact, only 12 percent of employees leave their job because they want more money.[3] And yet, in my very own firm, I extended a counteroffer now and then because I, too, thought the pain of an employee departing was simply too much for the company to bear at that time. Let me add that the few counteroffers I extended failed miserably. I should have let each of them go and known the company would have been better off for it.

One particular counteroffer was one of the worst decisions I ever made for my company. I had an employee who was extremely well-liked in her role as a director of one of our teams. She was good and competent but not great—I would say a C+ player. Her resignation came at a terrible time; I was right in the middle of confidentially selling the business. Had I stepped back, consulted my outside board members, and removed the emotions around this, I would have made the right decision and accepted her resignation, and the future health of the firm would have been much better.

I had a very competent second-in-command who deserved the promotion. She was more skilled and deserving of the role and did most of the customer management, new business development, and work in this division. Lucky for me, my second-in-command didn't get wind of the other employee's resignation, and our company was sold only a few months later. I am certain this situation would have had a very unhappy outcome if it weren't for the purchase of the firm.

Handcuffed by Emotion

The reasons I felt handcuffed into keeping this employee were purely emotional. Her resignation was very upsetting for me because she had been a consistent part of my company. Growing up, I yearned for consistency; each time someone left my firm, a little bit of me left with them.

I was also personally very invested in this employee. She really meant something to me; she had a background much like mine and had struggled with many similar issues growing up. Regardless of my personal feelings, I should have stepped back, sought outside guidance, and made the necessary transition to allow this employee to move on to her happy. Additionally, I missed the opportunity to promote a deserving, hardworking, tenured employee who rightfully should have received this promotion.

Build Out the Process

Resignations are tricky because you have a very limited amount of time to organize your decisions and direction before your entire organization finds out. And make no mistake, if one person knows, they all do. Get ahead of the communications and provide your employees with honest messaging. If you don't get the message out, your employees will be happy to form their own opinions.

Here's what should occur internally:

1. Create clear messaging to the immediate team and then to the entire company. This can be done in person through a town hall meeting or in an extremely well-written and thoughtful email announcement. I would recommend that the message to the immediate team be done in person by either yourself or their direct manager.

2. After the initial disruption, the position and workload will require immediate attention. Do you have a second-in-command or someone internally who would be suitable for this position? Look inside your firm before you seek outside sources. You will need to think

about temporarily delegating the workload or creating an interim process until you have a new hire on board.

3. Once you have created a road map, you need to immediately pivot to communication to your customers. This step is often missed when companies lose an employee. The dialogue and message should be managed by you. You don't want a customer to call and be surprised that their very important point of contact is no longer with the firm. This creates fear, doubt, and frustration. It can even cause your customers to leave! Create voicemail and email communications so that everything is clear and messages are forwarded to the correct personnel. Here is what a customer wants to hear:

   A. A positive message from a live person ensuring them that everything is fine and there will be no disruption in their level of service

   B. An introduction to their new or temporary point of contact, with reassurances that they are competent and know the account

4. Cross-reference all other locations to ensure the communication has been received and noted.

Start with Stay

You cannot be afraid of losing people. Your employees hear and see everything; do not think otherwise for even a moment. And when they find out a colleague of theirs does not want to work with them any longer or be a part of what they are working toward—and yet is being kept on—they become confused. They do not understand why you would want to keep someone who no longer believes in the mission of the company, and they often become disenchanted and resentful.

You might think you are doing a good thing by shielding your employees from the upset, but you are doing way more damage than good.

Once you get a resignation, it is too late. The work that needs to be done should take place long before a resignation occurs, to prevent it from ever happening.

Rather than focusing on the resignation, focus on preventing the resignation.

Stay meetings can potentially mitigate resignations, keep you ahead of the curve, and preserve your employees. You want your employees to be happy and flourish in their roles at your company. Stay meetings should be put into place to speak to your employees about their journey at your company. I do not mean your leaders meeting with their teams; I mean *you* meeting with them.

We discussed the importance of maintaining a review process and conducting either semi-annual or annual reviews, but it is critical to have additional points of contact with your employees throughout the year to ensure your employees remain engaged, challenged, happy, and excited to be working in your company. You will be surprised to find out how eager your employees are to meet with you, and you will most likely garner some very interesting feedback.

I found setting up quarterly stay meetings in twenty-minute increments one-on-one to be very effective. Since it might be uncharacteristic for you to meet directly with all your employees, start by letting them know the reason behind the request. Give them time to prepare for the meeting by providing a week or two of notice in the calendar invitation. We provided our employees with a series of questions we wanted them to answer as discussion points for our meeting.

Here are some suggestions for stay meeting questions:

1. Are there any talents or skills you would like to use that we aren't currently tapping into?

2. If you could change something about your job, what would it be?

3. What kind of feedback would you like to receive that you currently aren't getting?

4. Are there any areas where we could offer learning, training, or assistance to help you advance your skills and knowledge?

5. Does your job provide you with the flexibility you need to have a happy work-life balance?

6. Do you still feel fulfilled and happy in your current position?

7. Do you have any concerns or questions that you would like to share confidentially with me?

It is too late to have these conversations with your employees when a resignation comes. Having consistent stay meetings with your employees is necessary to ensure they are happy and completely engaged in your company. These meetings are a great way to identify issues early on, giving you time to potentially remedy problems and improve the retention of your employees. You will have a deeper understanding of your people, and they will deeply appreciate the time and effort you are putting into their well-being and their experience at the company.

The Final Interview

When resignations do happen, it is vital to conduct an exit interview. This is best done by your head of human resources, using a set of questions you have already created. Your hope is that each employee will be open and honest and help you learn about processes and situations within your firm that can be improved on. These exit interviews often provide great insight, and they should be copied to you so that you can remain informed about what is happening within your firm and make any changes you deem important. The ability to see trends, quickly recognize potential areas of concern, and stay ahead of issues are all part of being a great entrepreneur.

⌂ PUNCH LIST

- **Avoid counteroffers.** They are a temporary fix to a longer-term problem that needs to be addressed.

- **Let them go.** If an employee is motivated enough to go through the application and interview process elsewhere, they're done with their career at your firm, and they're ready to move on. Once someone has proposed working elsewhere, their old coworkers will view them with distrust. This hurts the team.

- **Communicate a departure.** After a team member leaves, be sure to do these things internally: tell the teams, sometimes in person; reconsider the position and work-load; give straight information to your customers so they're not taken by surprise; and make sure everyone has gotten the info.

- **Start with stay.** Conduct stay meetings to keep abreast of your employees' needs and your company's health. Listen to your employees before they decide to look for a position someplace else.

- **Finish with exit interviews.** This is best done by your head of human resources, using a set of questions you've already created. Your goal is to learn about processes and situations within your firm that can be improved on.

Empower Your People

"It is not the tools that you have faith in—tools are just tools—
they work, or they don't. It's the people you have faith in or not."

—STEVE JOBS

I am terrible when it comes to choosing paint colors. It is the one area where I fall short. Paint is like adding drapes to a room—it is a critical component for bringing the entire room to life. It also means you are getting close to the end. When choosing a paint color, you have to consider not only the room itself but the light or darkness of the space. Never judge a color sample in the store where you are buying it! Even a slight variation in color can change the rendering of a room and what you were hoping to achieve. Paint is a lot like storytelling—it adds zest, pop, and a completeness to it all. It's the great finisher.

Tell Me a Story

Salespeople are also excellent storytellers. They will present a compelling and extremely believable story to you each time they enter your office. The problem is, their gripping tale only represents one side of a two-sided story.

As a decision-maker, you will find that your employees regularly look to you to come up with solutions to all sorts of problems. When I started hearing stories at work, I'd listen to whichever side came to me first. I found myself agreeing with that side, and I made my decision. Only after many grueling months—and some really rotten decisions—did I realize I needed to always listen to *both* sides of the story before coming to a conclusion.

The last thing you want is a game of "whoever gets to the boss first will win the decision"! You have to make sure you are making *correct* decisions, or your people will become frustrated and disenchanted. Unfortunately, this can be complicated and time-consuming; there is nothing more challenging than handling a pressing issue by weaving together a solution as the facts trickle in, continually having to change your position.

Since we were in the people business, we had a lot of moving parts to our process. In some instances, a candidate might be represented by one division and staffing manager, and the customer by another. Many of our positions were crossover jobs, meaning job responsibilities often fell under two different divisions.

As an example, an office manager position brought to our firm for placement would be managed under our corporate services division. But if the office manager position required accounting and bookkeeping skills, this position could now also be managed by our accounting and finance division. This is where things got tricky. To best serve the customer, we would want one staffing manager as the point of contact for all the candidate submissions and direct conversations. Of course, each division and staffing manager had a compelling reason why they should represent this customer and what candidates should be presented. This was a minor problem but one that occurred often in our business.

The reality is, salespeople are often extremely reluctant to share the details of a customer with other team members. Salespeople forget that the customers actually belong to the company and should be shared by all verticals to provide the best customer experience. By sharing the customer with all members of your organization, you are ultimately providing them with the best possible solutions and services, which might not necessarily come from the original salesperson alone.

Put Trust in Your Team

It's best to put the decision-making responsibilities back on the management team whenever possible. By doing this, you are empowering and entrusting your people to use their good judgment and creative thinking to resolve issues. Remember in one of my earlier lessons I discussed the 4 Es—Execute, Entrust, Envelope, or Eliminate? You can apply this method to many of the daily issues that arise in business. Minor issues should be Entrusted to someone else. For extremely important issues that require your involvement, Execute on them yourself.

I had a competent group of managers but found that they got comfortable coming to me for all the answers. This not only prevented them from growing and working together, but also continually interrupted my day. People spend an average of eleven minutes on a project before they are interrupted. It takes them on average twenty-five minutes to get back to the point they were at before a distraction, according to a UC Irvine study.[1]

Having an open-door policy can become a crushing time suck if you don't properly manage your conversations and people issues. For me, it became so time-consuming I had to create some rules and measures to reclaim my time and manage my people. Here are some recommendations if you are losing control of your time in the office:

1. Start by setting expectations with each manager. Create time blocks to be available for issues, problems, and questions. Make sure that you also schedule "off-limit" times where you are not to be disturbed. Use a 5 p.m. or after-hours open-door policy so that you are free to discuss ideas with employees if needed. I recommend a later time so that employees stick around only for the important issues.

2. Move to an undisclosed space. When I had a project with a deadline that did not afford me any time for disruption, I moved to an undisclosed area. Your people will figure it out without you.

3. Make a rule that if someone brings a problem to you, they must bring two potential solutions as well. Get your people thinking!

4. Take a pause. People become accustomed to getting an answer quickly from you. It is important to pause and really think about the strategies and different solutions available. Also insist on gathering ideas from other employees. Your ideas won't always be the best ones!

5. When two people bring you a related issue, send them on their way to work it out themselves. This fosters

teamwork and collaboration and removes you completely from the decision.

One of the very best decisions I ever made was to reroute people whenever they came into my office with an issue. I would no longer discuss a problem if they didn't also propose at least one solution.

In most cases, your staff will know the answers; they are simply looking for validation. Sometimes collaborating and brainstorming on an issue can render the best solution.

It's important to stretch your people and allow them the opportunity to solve their own problems.

But when someone came to me to present an issue that involved another colleague, I turned them away. I would tell them I was grateful that they felt comfortable to discuss an issue, but they needed to resolve it directly with the other party involved.

Forced Change

Initially, my staff was uncomfortable with my new plan of action, and it took them a while to form the habit of coming up with a solution before they came to me. But soon they became accustomed to this process and no longer came into my office for these issues. Eventually, my groups started to work more cohesively and trust one another more, allowing me the time to do what I needed to do.

Because I reinforced my new process, employees took the time to come up with their own resolutions, which in turn built confidence and fostered teamwork. I cannot tell you how much time this new process returned to me and how uplifting it was to see my staff working out their own issues. Because I was not always immediately accessible, issues got resolved more quickly without my involvement, and staff members felt empowered to settle problems themselves and work more cohesively in teams.

Listen for the Quiet Ones

When running my business, I found that our people issues consumed about 30 percent of our days, and 10 percent of my people consumed 25 percent of my time. The larger your firm grows (both revenue and people), the more issues you will have to deal with daily. As I mentioned previously, I had a lot of the same people constantly seeking out my guidance. What I learned is that you can't ignore those employees who quietly and efficiently do their work, rarely causing any disruptions or seeking you out for feedback.

I had an employee who was with my firm for seventeen years. He was an exemplary employee, never causing any issues or problems, a superb cultural fit whom everyone adored. He saw the inside of my office less than ten times over the course of his seventeen-year career at our company! This employee was never part of the drama or the water cooler crowd; he just came in every day and did a great job. What I have come to realize is that this employee could have shared a different perspective with me on my company, and yet I didn't take the time to seek out his opinion.

When he resigned, I felt so disheartened, as the magnitude of him leaving and me not fully appreciating his stability, consistency, and work ethic all came crashing down into my reality. By creating processes like stay meetings within your organization, you will automatically be forced to connect and remain connected with your employees. Had we had this process in place, I might have been lucky enough to speak with him more often, gather valuable and insightful intel, and extend his career at my company.

⌂ PUNCH LIST

- **Protect your time.** When employees come to you with a story, be sure to listen to the other side before making a judgment.

- **Delegate decisions.** Sometimes delegating the decisions is a better use of your time. Trust your managers; after all, they're there for a reason.

- **Don't get caught in triangulation.** Give the decision-making authority back to your managers, and have them work together for a mutually beneficial solution.

- **Ask for resolutions.** If someone brings you a problem, have a rule that they must bring two potential solutions with them as well. Get your people thinking!

- **Block your time.** Make yourself unavailable, if you must, in order to force your staff to make decisions without you. This helps them feel empowered, and their decision-making skills will improve.

PART 7

The Final Product

The day has come. Touch-up is complete. You are screwing in your final wall plate, rolling out the carpets, and placing furniture in every room. All the months of setbacks, disappointments, budgetary constraints, time-lapses, inadequate crew members, and cash shortages are done. Things are gleaming, and you cannot help but step back, sigh, and say to yourself, "We are finally done!"

But are we?

Both in business and in home ownership, you are never done. There is critical maintenance that must continue, whether it be daily, weekly, monthly, or annually. You might find that your original idea didn't turn out exactly as you had envisioned, and modifications and improvements will need to occur. There will also be situations where something becomes obsolete or needs replacement.

In your business, some employees who started in a role may not be able to evolve as the company scales up; either they're no longer effective or they require additional training. What got you here won't get you there—which means you must elevate your staff and systems to get to the next level.

It is also critical to freshen up the paint every so often. Take a step back from your daily work and evaluate your people, your processes, and the direction in which your firm is headed to ensure everything is working as you had envisioned. You are never done. And you do not want to be.

You've Only Just Begun

"The ultimate measure of a man is not where he stands in moments of comfort and convenience, but where he stands at times of challenge and controversy."

—MARTIN LUTHER KING JR.

A s I finish up this book, I am a part of a world pandemic: COVID-19. Other than essential businesses, we are all under full quarantine. No one saw this coming, nor could they have prepared for such a catastrophic hit to our country. The pandemic had a major impact on small businesses and entrepreneurs throughout the US. I spent my first few weeks speaking to C-level executives and business owners, attending emergency roundtable meetings with my executive forum members, and watching webinars on management in crisis.

I have had the displeasure of witnessing people under duress and great anxiety before this pandemic. During my thirty-three years of leadership, there were plenty of times I was sick to my stomach over world issues that negatively affected our business. We managed to successfully navigate three recessions, Y2K, and 9/11, plus a myriad of other smaller issues that could have caused great harm to our firm.

Countless issues keep me—and maybe you—up at night: cybersecurity and disruption, talent shortages, a looming recession, political outcomes, and civil unrest, just to name a few. As a leader, you must always be prepared for the unexpected, maintain a calm and cool demeanor, and not buckle under pressure. Your number-one responsibility is to keep your people safe, protected, and well informed. Regardless of how you might feel on the inside, you must be courageous, honest, communicative, and collected when speaking with your people. Here is what I learned from the many crises my company navigated.

Your people look to you to be focused and calm when navigating uncharted waters. They need you to be an excellent communicator. In the absence of that, they will make up their own messaging and may completely unravel. As the president and governors did initially, you must speak to your people daily during crises. They need to physically see you.

As a leader, you must show up every day and act as a coach to your people.

A coach's job is to lay out a strategy for the team to follow. They must be succinct, create the vision, and then sell the vision to their team. And finally, they must be inspiring and believable, someone that people want to follow—no matter what obstacles lie in the path. Chaotic and uncertain times are when you must rally your people, provide facts, squelch rumors, and provide creative ideas and solutions.

And here is the greatest lesson of all, which comes in the form of a parable taken from Dan Heath's book *Upstream: The Quest to Solve Problems Before They Happen.* It goes something like this: Two friends are sitting by a river when they spot a child who is drowning in the water. Both friends immediately dive in and pull the child to safety. But as soon as they do, another struggling child drifts into view. Then another. Then another. After completing several more rescues, one of them climbs out of the water. "Where are you going?" the other friend asks. To this, the other friend responds, "I'm going upstream to tackle the guy who's throwing all of these kids in the water."

Most managers focus on attacking the symptoms—the kids—rather than the problem itself: whoever is throwing them in. Leaders focus on the vision, always looking ahead to create solutions to problems that have not happened yet. Managers have the ability to solve the problem at hand, whereas leaders have the foresight to remediate issues that have not yet occurred or that aren't apparent to others.

Additionally, it's one thing to formulate a great strategy and quite another to get your teams to adopt, enforce, and manage it to long-term continued success. It is especially difficult to implement a plan when you and your organization are under great duress and feeling anxious. One thing is for sure: After a crisis, you will know who your true leaders are and who your managers are, for there is a vast difference between managers and leaders. Those who are not leaders should not be in a position of such great importance.

After a childhood of struggles, dropping out of school, running a successful multimillion-dollar business, and building a life I am extremely proud of, there is still so much more to accomplish. As I finished this book, I opened my second start-up business in the middle of a pandemic and during a volatile presidential election year. I have been given the gift of time, as I spent the last few years unpacking all the lessons learned in my first business.

Yet as I continue with this new venture, I am certain that I will be fully committed to ensuring each member of my new company is fully devoted and aligned culturally. I will not tolerate negative detractors. To avoid retaining people who don't align with our mission, I will double down on my people-acquisition process. I will broaden my network of employees who have the courage and wisdom to contribute their opinions to the company and me, and I will enact change swiftly when needed. And for the several stellar employees who got away, I will seek you out in hopes that you will return to contribute your greatness to this new venture.

I am the foreman, the contractor who became a builder of her own business and took charge of her life—placing the footings, laying the foundation, adding the timbers, and ultimately creating a beautiful life and business for myself.

If you apply these best practices consistently, hire attitude over experience, and foster a culture that puts people first, you, too, can achieve remarkable results.

I hope this book has taught you that your people are your most important assets when building a "best in class" business.

I wish you much success on your entrepreneurial journey.

Appendix

I was lucky enough to find the original letter that my most profound mentor, Marian McIntyre (my godmother and aunt), wrote to me the day I landed my first job that started my professional career. Her constant words of support and reassurance continue to ring in my ears today; specifically, "You can be anything that set your mind to." I believe that everyone deserves the encouragement of an Aunt Marian, and I proudly share her words with you.

Here is her letter translated for easier reading:

Dearest Leslie—

Today is not only a happy day for you, but one for me also. I'm glad I was with you when you heard the wonderful news about your new job. I know you realize how important this is, because you did it all on your own. All my caring for you, loving you, and advising you—even arguing with you paid off and you hit the jackpot! Because you grew up to be the person that you are, you got your reward and rightfully so. You walked into that office and immediately sold yourself, as the lovely, intelligent person you have become. It isn't everyone who could do this, but it was so natural with you, they were very impressed. You see how important planning your life really is. To a certain extent we do make our own luck. You are only starting what should be a very meaningful, wonderful life . . . .

You have brought me more joy and happiness than anyone in this world besides Phil. Just seeing you so happy and confident today, I am content knowing you have grown up to be a mature, well-adjusted young woman. There is a price on everything we do in life and eventually we have to pay it. Today you got what was due you and it was beautiful, because you earned it. For the next ninety years it will always be the same if you make it that way. I'm so proud of you and love you more than I can ever say.

—M

Dearest Leslie—

Today is not only a happy day for you, but one for me also. I'm glad I was with you when you heard the wonderful news about your new job. I know you realize how important this is, because you did it all on your own. All my caring for you, loving you and advising you—even arguing with you paid off and you hit the jackpot! Because you grew up to be the person you are, you got your reward and rightfully so. You walked into that office and immediately sold yourself, as the lovely, intelligent person you have become. It isn't everyone who could do this, but it was so natural with you, they were very impressed. You see how important planning your life really is. To a certain extent we do make our own luck. You are only starting what should be a very meaningful, wonderful life.

My Favorite Renovations

Throughout this book I have incorporated many comparisons to construction. Building and remodeling are very comparable to scaling and growing a business. My two most recent renovations follow; projects that had many unforeseen setbacks and complications, yet turned out to be my most victorious and lucrative renovations to date.

CARLYNN

Before: With a little help from Hurricane Sandy, this gentle remodel became a complete renovation from the studs up.

After: Renovations occurred right after Hurricane Sandy in 2012. What started as a gentle remodel turned into razing the structure, remediating the contaminated soil, and leaving only two timbers of the original house.

Sunnieholme

Before: The moment we saw this lovely little yellow Cape Cod, we saw the vision of what was and could be once again. We restored this home, keeping its original character in mind, as it was part of the original Annie B. Jennings estate in 1939.

After: This renovation took a year and a half to complete, repurposing the excavated brick that was originally used for Annie B. Jennings's underground waterways for her expansive rose gardens. Mirroring her original carriage house sits a new barn and outdoor courtyard, completing and restoring the character of this wonderful home and the very place this book was completed.

Notes

PREFACE

1. Wagner, Eric T. "Five Reasons 8 out of 10 Businesses Fail." *Forbes*, 2 Sept. 2015, www.forbes.com/sites/ericwagner/2013/09/12/five-reasons-8-out-of-10-businesses-fail/?sh=6b8ecf826978.

LESSON 1

1. Fuller, Joseph B., and Manjari Raman. *Dismissed by Degrees: How Degree Inflation Is Undermining U.S. Competitiveness and Hurting America's Middle Class*. Harvard Business School, 2017.

2. Glassdoor Team. "50 HR & Recruiting Stats That Make You Think." *Glassdoor for Employers*, 21 Dec. 2018, www.glassdoor.com/employers/blog/50-hr-recruiting-stats-make-think/.

3. "55 Icebreaker Questions to Use When Meeting New People." *Indeed*, 10 Nov. 2020, www.indeed.com/career-advice/finding-a-job/icebreaker-questions-to-use-when-meeting-new-people.

4. Manager, Area Sales. "Airgas Regional Sales Manager Salaries in the United States." *Indeed*, www.indeed.com/cmp/Airgas/salaries/Regional-Sales-Manager.

5. Heinz, Kate. "42 Shocking Company Culture Statistics You Need to Know." *Built In*, 2 Oct. 2019, builtin.com/company-culture/company-culture-statistics.

6. James, Patrick. "How Much Data Do Americans Consume Each Day?" *GOOD*, 1 Aug. 2019, www.good.is/articles/how-much-data-do-americans-consume-each-day.

7. "How Much Is That Bad Hire Costing Your Business?" *CareerBuilder*, 16 Feb. 2020, resources.careerbuilder.com/recruiting-solutions/how-much-is-that-bad-hire-costing-your-business.

8. "Recruitment: What Do 79 Percent of Job Seekers Use to Find Their Next Role?" *Employee Benefits*, 13 Nov. 2019, employeebenefits.co.uk/recruitment-what-do-79-of-job-seekers-use-to-find-their-next-role/.

9. Ignatova, Maria. "56% of Professionals Rank Talent Brand as Top Factor When Picking a Job." *LinkedIn Talent Blog*, 1 Apr. 2014, business.linkedin.com/talent-solutions/blog/2014/04/employer-brand-stats.

LESSON 2

1. Lee, Dick, and Delmar Hatesohl. "Listening: Our Most Used Communications Skill." *University of Missouri Extension*, 1993, extension.missouri.edu/publications/cm150.

2. Cabrera, Beth. *Beyond Happy: Women, Work, and Well-Being.* Association for Talent Development Press, 2015.

3. Wholley, Meredith. "12 Diversity Statistics That Will Make You Rethink Your Hiring Decisions." *ClearCompany*, 13 Aug. 2020, blog.clearcompany.com/12-diversity-hiring-statistics-rethink-your-decisions.

4. Haden, Jeff, and Jennifer Carsen. "Why You Need an Employee Handbook for Your Small Business (Infographic)." *Gusto*, 6 Sept. 2019, gusto.com/blog/people-management/small-businesses-employee-handbooks-stand-infographic.

5. Peterson, Gary. "Three Reasons Why Values Matter, and I'm Not Talking the Money Kind." *Forbes*, 14 Aug. 2013, www.forbes.com/sites/garypeterson/2013/08/14/three-reasons-why-values-matter-and-im-not-talking-the-money-kind/?sh=8e14b801d936.

6. "CEOs and CFOs Share How Corporate Culture Matters." *Columbia Business School*, 15 Nov. 2017, www8.gsb.columbia.edu/newsroom/newsn/3874/ceos-and-cfos-share-how-corporate-culture-matters.

7. Heinz, Kate. "42 Shocking Company Culture Statistics You Need to Know." *Built In*, 2 Oct. 2019, builtin.com/company-culture/company-culture-statistics.

LESSON 3

1. Howes, Ryan. "Cool Intervention #10: The Miracle Question." *Psychology Today*, 18 Jan. 2010, www.psychologytoday.com/us/blog/in-therapy/201001/cool-intervention-10-the-miracle-question.

2. United States Congress, Mental Health America, et al. "Mind the Workplace." Mental Health America, 2017.

3. Schwantes, Marcel. "A New Study Reveals 70 Percent of Workers Say They Are Actively Looking for a New Job. Here's the Reason in 5 Words." *Inc.*, 4 Dec. 2018, www.inc.com/marcel-schwantes/a-new-study-reveals-70-percent-of-workers-say-they-are-actively-looking-for-a-new-job-heres-reason-in-5-words.html.

4. Human Capital Institute. "Statistics: Rethink Your Candidate Experience or Ruin Your Brand." *Human Capital Institute*, October 1, 2018, www.hci.org/blog/statistics-rethink-your-candidate-experience-or-ruin-your-brand.

LESSON 4

1. Stybel, Dr. Laurence J. "Why 33 Percent of New Employees Quit in 90 Days." *Psychology Today*, 3 Mar. 2019, www.psychologytoday.com/us/blog/platform-success/201903/why-33-percent-new-employees-quit-in-90-days.

2. Hirsch, Arlene S. "Don't Underestimate the Importance of Good Onboarding." *SHRM*, 30 July 2020, www.shrm.org/resourcesandtools/hr-topics/talent-acquisition/pages/dont-underestimate-the-importance-of-effective-onboarding.aspx.

3. CareerBuilder. "How Much Is That Bad Hire Costing Your Business?" *CareerBuilder*, 16 Feb. 2020, resources.careerbuilder.com/recruiting-solutions/how-much-is-that-bad-hire-costing-your-business

LESSON 5

1. "40+ HR and Recruiting Stats for 2020." *Glassdoor*, 2020, www.glassdoor.com/employers/resources/hr-and-recruiting-stats/.

2. Stafiej, Mike. "Employee Referral Statistics You Need to Know for 2020 (Infographic)," *LinkedIn*, 13 Jan. 2020, www.linkedin.com/pulse/employee-referral-statistics-you-need-know-2020-mike-stafiej/?articleId=6622562177335336961.

3. Lechter, Sharon L., and Greg S. Reid. *Three Feet from Gold: Turn Your Obstacles into Opportunities!* Sound Wisdom, 2020.

LESSON 6

1. Stevenson, Mason. "Bad Hiring Costs—By the Numbers." *HR Exchange Network*, 10 Jan. 2020, www.hrexchangenetwork.com/hr-talent-acquisition/articles/poor-hiring-costs-by-the-numbers.

2. Anderson, Merrill C. "Added Value." *Viking Principle*, 2018, www.vikingprinciple.com/added-value-of-coaching.

LESSON 7

1. Clay, Robert. "Why You Must Follow Up Leads." *Marketing Donut*, www.marketingdonut.co.uk/sales/sales-techniques-and-negotiations/why-you-must-follow-up-leads.

2. Rogers, Stewart. "Those Incredible Sales Stats Everyone Cites Are Actually Completely False." *VentureBeat*, 13 July 2018, venturebeat.com/2014/08/15/these-incredible-sales-stats-everyone-cites-are-actually-completely-false/.

3. Hadfield, Ryan. "53 Sales Follow Up Statistics." *ZoomInfo*, 12 Oct. 2020, blog.zoominfo.com/sales-follow-up-statistics/.

4. Mansfield, Matt. "Customer Retention Statistics—The Ultimate Collection for Small Business." *Small Business Trends*, 21 Apr. 2020, smallbiztrends.com/2016/10/customer-retention-statistics.html.

5. Williams, Brian. "21 Mind-Blowing Sales Stats." *Brevet Blog*. thebrevetgroup.com/21-mind-blowing-sales-stats.

LESSON 8

1. Williams, Brian. "21 Mind-Blowing Sales Stats." *Brevet Blog*. thebrevetgroup.com/21-mind-blowing-sales-stats.

2. Kulbytė, Toma. "Customer Retention: 5 Unique Strategies to Increase Profits." *SuperOffice*, 4 Nov. 2020, www.superoffice.com/blog/customer-retention-tips-with-crm-software/

3. Mansfield, Matt. "Customer Retention Statistics—The Ultimate Collection for Small Business." *Small Business Trends*, 21 Apr. 2020, smallbiztrends.com/2016/10/customer-retention-statistics.html.

LESSON 9

1. Palmer, Barbara. "How to Express Gratitude at Work." *PCMA*, 6 Nov. 2018, www.pcma.org/gratitude-workplace/.

2. Hyman, Jeff. "To Attract the Best, First Understand Why They Leave." *Forbes*, 19 Aug. 2020, www.forbes.com/sites/jeffhyman/2018/05/09/whytheyleave/?sh=7c3088853486.

3. Gibbons, Serenity. "You and Your Business Have 7 Seconds to Make a First Impression: Here's How to Succeed." *Forbes*, 20 June 2018, www.forbes.com/sites/serenitygibbons/2018/06/19/you-have-7-seconds-to-make-a-first-impression-heres-how-to-succeed/?sh=33322c2a56c2.

4. Shannon, Polly. "First Impressions—The 7/11 Rule." *Positive Business DC*, 27 Oct. 2015, positivebusinessdc.com/711-rule/.

LESSON 11

1. Doran, G. T. "There's a S.M.A.R.T. Way to Write Management's Goals and Objectives." *Management Review*, vol. 70, no. 11, 1981, pp. 35–36.

LESSON 12

1. McGovern, Joy et al. "Maximizing the Impact of Executive Coaching." *The Manchester Review*, vol. 6, no. 1, 2001.

2. Staats, Bradley R. "Don't Just Dive into Action: Stop to Think First." *Wall Street Journal*, 6 July 2018, www.wsj.com/articles/dont-just-dive-into-action-stop-to-think-first-1530888843.

3. Wetmore, Donald E. E. "Time Management Facts and Figures." *The Productivity Institute*, 2018, www.balancetime.com/2018/12/time-management-facts-and-figures/.

4. "Executive Coaching & Team Building." *Performance Partners*, www.ppartners.com/services/executive-team-building.

5. "Business Coaching Statistics." *Monte Wyatt*, 2019, www.monte-wyatt.com/services/business-coaching-statistics/.

6. G, Deyan. "17+ Little-Known Time Management Statistics For 2020." *TechJury*, 28 July 2020, techjury.net/blog/time-management-statistics/.

7. Finkel, David. "New Study Shows You're Wasting 21.8 Hours a Week." *Inc.*, 1 Mar. 2018, www.inc.com/david-finkel/new-study-shows-youre-wasting-218-hours-a-week.html.

8. Bregman, Peter. "Consider Not Setting Goals in 2013." *Harvard Business Review*, 2 Feb. 2018, hbr.org/2012/12/consider-not-setting-goals-in.html.

9. James, Geoffrey. "You Simply Won't Believe How Much Time You Waste in Meetings at Work, According to MIT." *Inc.*, 23 Sept. 2019, www.inc.com/geoffrey-james/you-simply-wont-believe-how-much-time-you-waste-in-meetings-at-work-according-to-mit.html.

10. G., Deyan. "20+ Little-Known Time Management Statistics For 2020." *TechJury*, 28 July 2020, techjury.net/blog/time-management-statistics/.

11. Rakicevic, Mira. "27 Meditation Statistics That You Should Be Aware Of." *DisturbMeNot!*, 4 June 2020, disturbmenot.co/meditation-statistics/.

12. "Top 22 Meditation Statistics Reveal Data and Trends for 2019." *The Good Body*, 13 Feb. 2020, www.thegoodbody.com/meditation-statistics/.

LESSON 13

1. "Understanding the Stages of Change." *The Change Companies*, 25 June 2019, www.changecompanies.net/blog/stages-of-change/.

2. "The Stages of Change." *Virginia Tech*, doi:https://www.cpe.vt.edu/gttc/presentations/8eStagesofChange.pdf

3. Goldman, Jeremy. "Here's How Much Your Bad Employees Are Costing You." *Inc.*, 8 June 2016, www.inc.com/jeremy-goldman/here-s-how-much-your-bad-employees-are-costing-you.html.

LESSON 14

1. "Hiring Guide for 2020 Recovery: Reimagine Recruiting and Retention." *TalenTrust*, 2020, p. 6., doi:https://talentrust.com/hiring-guide/?cn-reloaded=1.

2. Schomer, Stephanie. "He Asked His Team How to Avoid Layoffs. Their Response Thrilled Him." *Entrepreneur*, 4 Dec. 2020, www.entrepreneur.com/article/359946.

3. Schomer. "He Asked His Team How to Avoid Layoffs. Their Response Thrilled Him."

LESSON 15

1. "Where Culture Meets People." *Culpeo* HR, 2020, www.culpeohr.com.

LESSON 16

1. "2018 ReviewTrackers Online Reviews Stats and Survey." *ReviewTrackers*, 1 July 2020, www.reviewtrackers.com/reports/online-reviews-survey/.

2. Votaw, Kathleen Quinn. *Solve the People Puzzle: How High-Growth Companies Attract & Retain Top Talent.* Advantage, 2016.

3. Lardieri, Alexa. "Ford to Lay Off 7K Workers in Effort to Cut Costs." *U.S. News & World Report*, 20 May 2019, www.usnews.com/news/economy/articles/2019-05-20/ford-to-lay-off-7k-workers-in-effort-to-cut-costs.

4. Goldman, Jeremy. "Here's How Much Your Bad Employees Are Costing You." *Inc.*, 8 June 2016, www.inc.com/jeremy-goldman/here-s-how-much-your-bad-employees-are-costing-you.html.

LESSON 17

1. Cross, Stuart. "The Five C's of Leading in Adversity." *CBS News*, 23 Sept. 2008, www.cbsnews.com/news/the-five-cs-of-leading-in-adversity/.

LESSON 18

1. Wren, Jay. "Job Counter Offers: The Stress of Leaving a Company." *Jay Wren*, 26 Sept. 2017, www.jaywren.com/job-counter-offers/.

2. "Top 10 Reasons Not to Accept a Job Counteroffer." *Surf Search*, 2 Nov. 2018, surfsearch.org/jobseeker-resources/counter-offers/.

3. Nordstrom, Todd and David Stuart. "10 Shocking Workplace Stats You Need to Know." *Forbes*, 8 Mar. 2018, www.forbes.com/sites/davidsturt/2018/03/08/10-shocking-workplace-stats-you-need-to-know/?sh=6abc19d0f3af.

LESSON 19

1. Mark, Gloria, et al. "The Cost of Interrupted Work: More Speed and Stress." University of California, Irvine, 2008, www.ics.uci.edu/~gmark/chi08-mark.pdf.

LESSON 20

1. Heath, Dan. *Upstream: The Quest to Solve Problems Before They Happen*. Avid Reader Press, 2020.

About the Author

Leslie McIntyre-Tavella has devoted her entire career to people: counseling them, placing them in life-changing opportunities, and providing "best in class" talent to customers who pride themselves on "people first." Leslie developed these skills by cultivating a culture that fostered teamwork and comradery, and she retained her employees twice as long as the industry standard. Finding, hiring, and retaining the right people is the secret sauce to building a solid foundation and the winning ingredient needed to succeed wildly!

Leslie launched her first start-up organization thirty years ago to bring a different service paradigm to the recruiting and staffing industry. Her prior company became a $20 million company and won numerous awards, including first place in "Best Places to Work" and eleventh place for the top "Women-Owned Businesses in Connecticut." Leslie is a progressive leader and entrepreneur who's comfortable collaborating and engaging with C-suite executives in a wide range of industries. She has held leadership and membership roles in various industry groups, including a board position at Dress for Success and chairman for the Connecticut chapter of the American Staffing Association. Leslie has also written for several periodicals and magazines.

After three years away from the staffing industry, Leslie realized that her perspective had shifted to reveal new insights on where the gaps are today in HR and optimization, customer engagement, culture and team alignment, and talent acquisition. Leslie's new start-up focuses on managed services for human resources, customer engagement, and teaching firms how to optimize their talent pipeline. Culpeo HR, where culture meets people, partners with small businesses to enhance people, production, performance, and profitability.

When Leslie is not spending time innovating and addressing customers' needs, she is busy renovating homes, condos, and office buildings. She loves taking something that is shabby and rundown and giving it a new life. Leslie just finished her thirteenth renovation—a farmhouse and barn in Fairfield, Connecticut, where she currently resides with her husband.

When time permits, she can be found hitting the trails at Stratton Mountain, where she is a black diamond skier. Leslie is a big-time lover of Goldendoodles, black coffee, and gardening, and she thoroughly enjoys time with her family and close friends.